TRAGIC TRAIN

"The City of San Francisco"

The finest streamliner ever designed began regular service between San Francisco and Chicago on January 2, 1939. This photograph was taken of her 11 cars in the high Sierras of California when the train rolled eastward on her trial run. She is on the westward track near Long Ravine trestle between Colfax and Cape Horn on a 10° 00′ curve.

TRAGIC TRAIN

"The City of San Francisco"

By

Don DeNevi

129582

Superior PUBLISHING COMPANY

Library of Congress Cataloging in Publication Data

DeNevi, Donald P.
Tragic train, "the City of San Francisco".

Includes index.
1. Southern Pacific Railroad. 2. Railroads —
United States — Express-trains. I. Title.
TF25.S72D46   364.1'64   77-3499
ISBN 0-87564-525-9

FIRST EDITION

Printed and Bound in Canada by Evergreen Press, Ltd.,
Vancouver, B.C.

A SMALL TRIBUTE

For the first time, this story is being told in its entirety. Hopefully, someone somewhere will be moved to step forward with new evidence, or a confession, to help solve the case.

If there is to be a dedication to this book, it should serve as a recognition of those hundreds of special agents who so laboriously searched for the murderers. These determined and courageous men have not been forgotten.

Perhaps their efforts will not have been in vain.

TABLE OF CONTENTS

OTHER BOOKS BY DON DeNEVI

Sketches of Early California

Portraits of America's Universities

Five Heritages: Teaching Multi-Cultural Populations

Racism In 19th Century America

Muckrakers and Robberbarons

Tricks and Puzzles of the 19th Century

Alcatraz 46 — The Anatomy Of A Classic Prison Tragedy

Four Against the Rock (Edited for Clarence Carnes)

Western Train Robberies

Roy, California's Nicest Badman

Earthquakes: Our Tortured Planet

Our Changing Climate

An Illustrated History of The Western Pacific Railroad

Railroad Detective

The Humanization of Space: The Ultimate Migration (in Progress)

Champ Champlin as a young special agent. O'Connell assigned him to investigate possible leads in Oregon and northern California. Today, Champlin is Chief Special Agent for Southern Pacific.

FOREWORD
by
Clarence "Champ" Champlin
Chief Special Agent-System, Southern Pacific
Transportation Company

The story you are about to read is not just another train thriller.

Unfortunately, it is true and concerns one of the most dastardly acts of sabotage in American railroad history. Although the case is nearly 40 years old, it has not been forgotten by any means. And, I would like to call to the reader's attention that a $10,000 reward is still open for information leading to an arrest and conviction.

Although there were over a hundred streamlined trains in regular service across America during 1939, the $2,000,000 City of San Francisco was not just another stylish, aerodynamically profiled diesel-engined train. To the Southern Pacific Company, she was the pride of the fleet, an appropriate symbolic form for the modernization of rail travel. To those of us in the company, she was the most exciting train of the decade and her service was incomparable. Synchronizing flashing speed with the luxury of an ultra-modern hotel, she carried 171 passengers and could travel the distance between Chicago and the Golden Gate in 39 hours and 15 minutes.

Her story is now told publicly for the first time. With the case remaining open, Southern Pacific has always turned away prospective authors or Hollywood script writers who wished to describe in words or with film the derailment and subsequent manhunt.

Now, in order to once again spur interest in the sabotage, Southern Pacific has given Don DeNevi permission to review the evidence and record the details. Utilizing confidential company records, along with the still living survivors, he has written an intelligent and readable account of one of the most determined manhunts of the 20th century. Not only does his efforts provide us with fresh and consistently well-written perspectives, but this valuable book also testifies to DeNevi's maturity as an authoritative historian. Everyone from the most serious railroad buff to the general mystery fan will appreciate what Southern Pacific railroad detectives endured during those search years.

Perhaps the story will bring forth some new evidence. If so, please contact me immediately. Nothing would please me more than to break open the case in the memory of Dan O'Connell, Chief Special Agent for Southern Pacific, who devoted the remaining 12 years of his life in pursuing the trainwreckers.

The head end of the streamliner is seen on the westward track about seven rail lengths from Horseshoe Curve near Palo Alto, California. The degree of the curve is 9° 46′. Note the head of the engineer.

Chapter 1

THE CITY OF
SAN FRANCISCO

"As modern as tomorrow, embodying spaciousness and refinements never before available to passengers, the mighty streamliner, named after the metropolis at her western terminus, is truly a press agent's dream train. There's plenty to write about in bold exclamations. Every thing is the finest, the last word in distinctive passenger car design, ultra in the nicety of its appointments, sensational in minute attention to the smallest details. In fact, the whole train is colossal in conservative use of Hollywood parlance!"

Such was the ecstatic press release from the Southern Pacific Company when the City of San Francisco was inaugurated on January 2, 1938. Known as the world's most superlative train, she was promoted as the "largest, fastest, most beautiful, powerful, and luxurious streamliner ever designed." With brilliant reddish brown and orange motifs in bold relief against a silver background, she was the holiday gift to transcontinental travelers because her run from Chicago to San Francisco was only 39½ hours.

To engineering design experts, there was little question that she was the most awesome passenger train ever conceived.

For example, the power units consisted of the longest locomotive ever built, 210 feet long. As far as the coaches were concerned, the City of San Francisco had been assigned 17 instead of the 11 found in conventional models. Thus, her length was 1,292 feet, just short of a quarter of a mile.

Her six giant engines in the three power cars were the most powerful Diesel locomotive engines the world had ever known. There had never been anything like them before. They generated 5400 horsepower as compared with 2400 in the smaller passenger trains of Southern Pacific.

The Winton 900-horsepower, 12 cylinder, two-cycle, V-type Diesel engines used to drive the streamliner were the first of their types used in American railroad passenger service. With 8-inch by 10-inch cylinders, each individual engine was designed to develop the 900 horse powers at 750 revolutions per minute. Compared to the conventional 600 horse powers of 1,200 r.p.m., the earlier engines installed on the first Southern Pacific high speed passenger trains had been designed to operate by the distillate-burning method. In the latest version, a single Diesel engine was 20 feet in overall length and weighed 18,000 pounds. The main generator weighed 11,700 pounds, while the driving motor weighed 26,400 pounds. The weight of the entire power plant, including engines, generator, motors, auxiliary engines, generator sets, pumps, radiators, air compressors, etc., was approximately 79,000 pounds.

Special features in the design of the Diesel engine included a cylinder block and crank case made entirely of rolled steel plate welded into one piece. The main frame work of each engine was one solid piece to which a light oil pan, cast iron cylinder heads, and other accessories were attached. Cylinder liners were of hard cast iron pressed into the welded steel framework and could be replaced without difficulty. In fact, all wearing parts of each engine were easily replaceable, thus promoting longer engine life. The cylinder heads had the innovation of smaller valves inserted in those heads. The exhaust connections had an individual pipe for each cylinder and protruded vertically between the cylinders. The pistons were of aluminum alloy and the connecting rods were of H-section drop forgings of alloy steel.

The electrical equipment consisting of a General Electric generator and four traction motors and

The City of San Francisco power units. The streamliner was jointly owned by Southern Pacific, Union Pacific, and Chicago North Western.

control had been especially designed for this specific power plant. The generator which was directly connected to the engine carried a built in exciter designed in such a way that the current demands of the traction motors regulated the amount of generator voltage. In this manner, the load on the engine was constant at any car speed and solely under the control of the engine throttle. Rated at 300 hp each, the traction motors were mounted two on each truck of the power car, and geared to the wheels.

An auxiliary generator unit, consisting of a 4-cycle, 5-inch by 7-inch 2-cycle oil engine directly connected to a 220-volt AC generator, was provided to furnish power for all the auxiliaries, controls, lights, air-conditioning equipment, heaters, pumps, etc. This auxiliary engine was of the same general construction as the main engine. The electric system throughout the streamliner used 220-volt 3-phase currents for all motors of ¼ horse-

power and over, and 32-volts for the lights and motors under ¼ horsepower. In short, each current was transmitted to the two traction motors mounted on each truck unit. Thus, the total prime mover and power transmitting equipment consisted of the six 900 hp Diesel engines and the six 600-volt generators with their 12 traction motors. The power was therefore applied to the rails at 24 different wheel points. Each power unit carried 1,100 gallons of boiler water and 1,200 gallons of ordinary fuel oil, the type burned in an ordinary household oil-burner. Under normal operating conditions the locomotive consumed approximately four gallons of fuel per mile at an average speed of 75 miles per hour, although her speed often ranged up to 110 miles an hour.

Other power equipment of the train which generated power for the lighting, heating, air-conditioning, telephones, radios, etc., was located in the auxiliary-baggage-dormitory car just be-

The City of San Francisco in preparation for her maiden voyage to Chicago.

hind the locomotive units. As mentioned, this equipment consisted of two EMC 450 hp Diesel-electric units operating in multiple to supply the 220 volt, 3 phase, 60 cycle alternating current, and could generate sufficient electricity to supply the needs of a fair sized town. The AC power supply was supplemented by a monstrous storage battery (710 A.H.) of 32 cells, or 64 volts, which was used for auxiliary apparatus control circuits and emergency lighting in the event of failure of both auxiliary power plants. Battery charging was by means of a small 12 kw motor generator set driven by power for the AC supply lines.

The power cars weighed fully equipped 163,040 pounds, or 31,800 pounds on the front truck and 81,240 pounds on the second. With such tonnage up

front, there was little question whether the streamliner would fly of the track. In addition, the total 530 tons without load guaranteed a smooth ride, although a certain rolling and pitching would be inevitable.

The bed for the main and auxiliary engines was formed of two aluminum plate girders, which extended from the rear end sill of the car to the front end, and was framed into the floor construction of the front end. The floor-line construction formed the center of the curved front end while all of the sectional members converged to form a strong parabolic arch which would resist any damage from possible collisions at highway crossings. Provision for the application and removal of the main Diesel engines and other large pieces of equipment

11

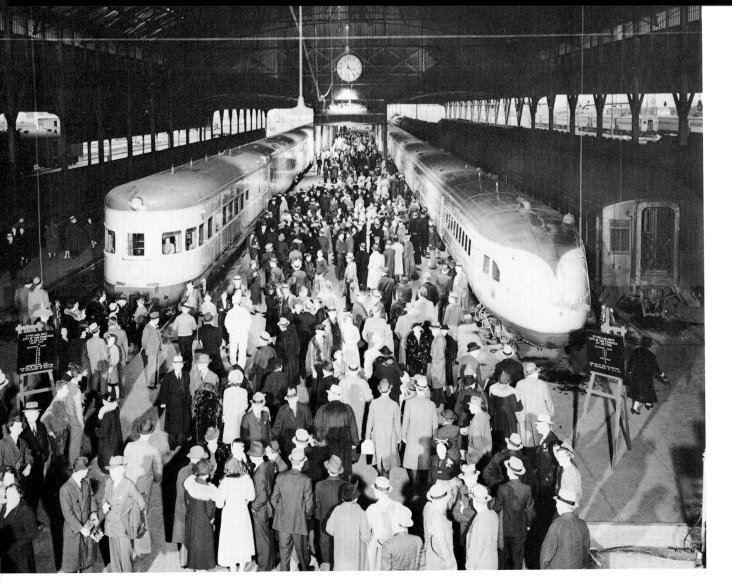

The City of San Francisco held an open house prior to her maiden voyage on January 2, 1938. More than 6,000 people were on hand for the inauguration. The original streamliner which had been in operation since 1936 is shown on the adjacent track to the right. Although the first City was a highly successful innovation, she was not altogether satisfactory from an aesthetic viewpoint. Like so many exploratory streamliners in the dawning years of the diesel, the valuable Pullman solarium and observation space in the last car was wasted on a coach-buffet of teardrop design with a blind rear end. The observation lounges of the second City of San Francisco were in great favor with travelers until World War II when they were removed as non-revenue luxury equipment.

The interior of the power car.

The inauguration of the City of San Francisco.

in the power car had been developed to suit the requirements of the streamliner. The superstructure of the car was removable at the side and end sills and by removing the fastenings at the sills. Thus, the entire superstructure could be lifted free from the underframe and apparatus deck.

All trucks of the train were of the four-wheel type, with welded frames of high-tensile steel. Each had rolled-steel wheels and axles. All the cars were constructed of aluminum alloy except for the two power units which were made of special high tensile steel. Having a tensile strength twice that of ordinary steel, the 17 cars weighed in at 1,207,251 pounds, or 30% less than that of ordinary type steel coaches and engines. The first two trucks had 36-inch wheels, equipped with roller bearings placed outside in order to provide space necessary for the driving motors. The armatures were also on roller bearings, having been wound for high maximum speed. The remaining five trucks had 33-inch rolled-steel wheels and inside-type roller-bearing journals to reduce the truck width and minimize air resistance. All roller bearings were liberally oversized for weight and speed requirements.

Further, the air-brake equipment for the City of San Francisco had been especially designed and built by the New York Air Brake Company. Featuring the use of the newly invented Decelakron control which had been created to assure stopping from exceptionally high speeds within the same distances of conventional passenger trains, Southern Pacific could boast of safety controls functioning as simply as those of an automobile. And, for extra safety, the streamliner had been designed with a low center of gravity by cutting down on her height without the slightest discomfort to passengers. Equipped with dual fog-

penetrating headlights, special brakes for high-speed deceleration, and the unusual color schemes which could be seen at great distances, the City of San Francisco symbolized the ultimate in safety engineering devices.

Equal to these engineering feats were other details of genius. For example, there were twin electrical outlets of 110 and 32 volts in all roomettes and wash rooms for electric shavers and curling irons. Even the dental lavatory had a foot pedal mechanism. Roomettes were so designed as to become private parlors in daytime, with beds that folded into the wall or became comfortable divans. Upholstered chairs would be collapsed and slipped under the beds at night. Broad double windows gave clear views. They were fog-proof, with outer panes of plate glass and inner panes of safety glass.

There was a great deal of difference in the streamliner's construction compared to conventional trains. For example, she had wider and higher cross sections, straight car sides instead of tapered, wider window openings in the lounge rooms, and she eliminated the single unit articulation of the entire train. Seven cars were separate while the others were articulated (connecting ends joined on the same wheel trucks) in pairs. This new arrangement facilitated handling the equipment in making repairs and also made it possible to extract certain cars in an emergency without delaying the whole train. Specially designed couplings, however, with rubber cushion draft gear assured smooth riding. And, rubber diaphragms held the cars snug in order to give the train an exterior appearance of being one unit.

In terms of cars and coaches, the streamliner consisted of compartments for baggage; the auxiliary power units and dormitory for dining car crew; one 54-seat chair car; an articulated two-

13

During the open house, many thousands of Bay Area citizens inspected the new streamliner. The people in the following photographs have never been identified.

unit diner, one full car seating 72 and the other seating 32, with kitchen and serving pantry between; one finely equipped club car seating 30; two 4-compartment and 3-drawing room cars, each articulated with a 12-section regular sleeping car; one 11-bedroom car, also articulated with a 12-section standard Pullman; one "roomette" car with 18 enclosed private rooms; one "duplex" with 5 double bedrooms and 12 single bedrooms; and a beautiful observation-lounge car with seats for 36, also equipped with a barbershop and small bar to supplement the main one in the club car, plus a private room for the stewardess-nurse and a facility for emergency medical attention, including an extra berth for use by a patient if necessary. This 84 feet, 6 inch car was said to be the longest passenger car ever built in the United States.

Some of the cars appropriately carried the names of San Francisco's famed centers of attraction such as Market Street, Presidio, Mission Dolores, Nob Hill, and Embarcadero. The sleeping cars were given such names as Twin Peaks, Fisherman's Wharf, Chinatown, Golden Gate Park, Union Square, Seal Rock, Telegraph Hill, and Portsmouth Square.

Costing over $2,000,000, the average cost per passenger was less than 2¢ a mile.

Sleeping car space was double that of conventional passenger trains, 168 berths compared to 84. Chair car space was increased to 54, totaling accommodations for 222 instead of 170. She had 60 compartments, drawing rooms, bedrooms, and "roomettes" instead of the regular 9. On board, she had a larger variety of sleeping accommodations to choose from than on any train in America. And, extra fare was only $15 in Pullman accommodations and $5 in the chair car. Pullman charges were the same as on other trains, but the fare for one of

the novel roomettes was $22.05 between Chicago and San Francisco.

Cars were broader and higher than on other passenger trains. Berths were 2½ inches wider and 1½ inches longer than in standard Pullmans, and there were even several extra long berths for tall individuals. Lounging and dining spaces were greatly enlarged and passengers and crew had the convenience of the most extensive telephone system ever installed on a train.

The roomette was a car entirely new in design. Each of the 18 private rooms was equipped with all the necessary facilities for long travel comfort. During the day, the bed folded into the wall and the passenger had available a comfortable sofa seat and lounge chair. The sliding door of the roomette could be locked at night, or left open and a curtain drawn across the opening. These rooms were completely air-conditioned, as were all the other passenger cars.

Other accommodations included windows in all the upper berths; radio reception throughout the train, with outlets in every room, plus compartments for portable set use; and, telephone systems so passengers could communicate service requests directly from rooms and other cars to the diner, club, and bar in the lounge car. The low priced meals served in your roomette or seat now made carrying of box lunches on board obsolete. In reality, you could eat your way across the continent at the rate of 90¢ a day — 25¢ for breakfast, 30¢ for luncheon, and 35¢ for a substantial excellently cooked and smoothly served three-course dinner. The diner-lounge and buffet kitchens in the coaches offered the most modern catering devices and service on wheels. Throughout the kitchen area, the latest scientific culinary hardware had been provided.

Mr. and Mrs. Grover Magnin, along with their son, were among the first passengers on the maiden voyage of the City of San Francisco. Grover Magnin is the owner of the fashionable woman's clothing store, I. Magnin's, in downtown San Francisco.

The Templeton and Stanford University track teams also accompany the streamliner on her maiden voyage.

In the observation-lounge car Nob Hill.

A traveling cocktail bar was permanently added as a regular part of the City of San Francisco. Although designed in a snappily, current decorative motif, plans were already underway to create a new "Frontier Shack" effect, the atmosphere of an old-time Western groggery. Although this car was also air-conditioned and illuminated by the latest in concealed fixtures, the idea was to design an interior to carry you back to the mining camps of 1849.

Indeed, all the interiors of the City of San Francisco had been planned by the best possible interior designers. With an architectural background made interesting by textured types of wall materials and by the simplicity of mouldings, the decorative effect was gained through the use of such colors as Nantes blue, apricot, smoke grays, jonquil yellows, beige tans, and French greens contrasted with complementary colors in seat coverings and general furnishings. All the fabrics were

of special weave and colors created for the train. For the first time, their designs were bolder and more striking than appeared on previous streamliners.

Ceiling lighting systems gracefully followed the contours of the large rooms in the main cars, adding effectively to their architectural schemes. In the reading zones, the glareless lights gave soft and full illumination.

Different types of finishes for hardware, mouldings, and furnishings were particularly new and noteworthy because up to 1938 all metal surfaces had been finished in satin aluminum. Now, the introduction of new metals offered such finishes as copper for the main diner and light brass in the club car. All the passenger cars had been built by the Pullman-Standard Car Manufacturing Company in Chicago and the power cars constructed by the Electro-Motive Corporation, a subsidiary of General Motors in LaGrange, Illinois.

In the dining car.

Interior of the coffee shop which was articulated.

But Southern Pacific was especially proud of the streamliner's extensive telephone system with separate circuits for passengers and car attendants, as well as for the train crew. This was indeed an outstanding engineering feature. Dial phones of the handset type were permanently installed in the club, dining, and coach of the sleeping cars, as well as the observation lounge. In addition, each sleeping car with compartments, drawing rooms, or double bedrooms, was equipped with portable phones which could be obtained from car porters and plugged into the room's jack. Passengers or porters could then call the stewards in the club and dining cars in order to place orders or make table reservations. Over the same system, the stewards could return calls in order to announce vacant reservation seats, or to question orders for meals or refreshments. Only one call could take place over the line at a given time and it was impossible for the conversation to be heard through any other telephone in the system. If the line was busy, no dial tone could be heard by the person initiating the call. Calls could not be made between passenger accomodations. However, at main passenger terminals, a special phone in the observation-lounge car could be connected so that passengers could call outside numbers.

Of special significance, the train telephone system allowed members of the crew to talk with the engineer, supplementing the traditional engineer's air signal. Handset phones were installed in the cab, 2nd and 3rd power cars, baggage car, diner, and observation-lounge. Calls, however, could not be initiated from the engineer's cab.

Another proud feature that Southern Pacific boasted about was the facility for radio reception throughout the train. In the chair car, main diner, coffee shop, and club cars, built-in 15-tube sets and loud speakers were controlled by car attendants. In the observation-lounge car, there was a 15-tube console set, and all drawing rooms and compartments had outlets for portable radios which passengers could bring with them or that could be obtained from attendants aboard the train.

The "For Women Only" section of the lounge coach was still another City of San Francisco innovation. A special train stewardess was responsible for this car in order that ladies could lounge in kimonos, nurse their babies in privacy, and in general let their hair down without even the train crew allowed to peek in.

The train stewardess had made her bow for the first time on the new streamliner. Like her sister on the 1939 aeroplane, she was a graduate nurse and appeared in a single, comfortable uniform. With her headquarters in the observation-lounge, her most important priority was attending women with babies. Southern Pacific was proud in boasting that "she is a mistress of the art of making the grouchiest mother and father happy and comfortable." With her exterior color scheme consisting of Armour Yellow from top to bottom, broadly striped by two wide bands of scarlet on both sides of the full length of the train, the City of San Francisco was without question the pride of the Southern Pacific fleet.

Interior of the tavern car.

Interior of the diner St. Francis Woods.

The ingenious "roomette" compartment especially designed for the City of San Francisco with wardrobe, easy lounging chair, spacious sofa, and other facilities for comfort day and night travel. The folding bed permitted more space for day use. Two lounge chairs were folded up at night and placed under the sofa-bed.

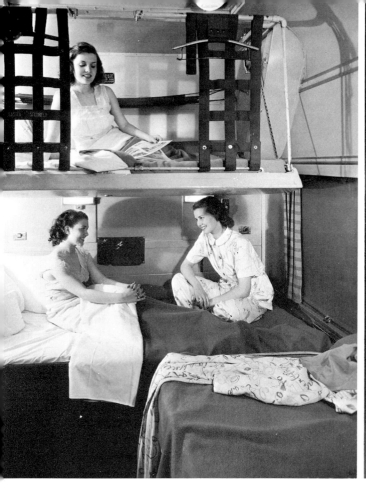
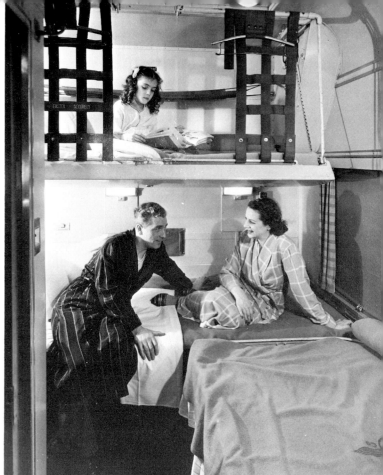

A group of passengers relaxing in the last car of the streamliner. Sofas and rotating chairs in this car and the adjoining parlor car were constructed of sponge rubber cushioning. Many combinations of harmonious colorings were used throughout the train with no two patterns or schemes identical.

★ ★ ★

After gazing out of his compartment window for some early morning color from the distant, bleak metropolis, the young man leaned back exhausted. After a sleepless night's journey of frequent stops and starts along isolated milk junctions between New York and Illinois, he was delighted the passenger train was at last streaking along at 60 miles per hour across the crooked river delta of Lake Michigan. Having been eliminated in the quarterfinals of the U.S. Open Tennis Tournament at Forest Hills, Tony Firpo was on the first stretch of his way home to Oakland, California. By taking the cheapest form of transportation to Chicago, he had saved enough to afford a seat on the luxurious transcontinental City of San Francisco streamliner which would make the trip in 39½ hours. Having seen a colorful advertisement in The Saturday Evening Post which described the new train, friendly service, and scenic overland route to California, he was determined to go home in the height of style.

Now, slicing into Chicago from Indiana on a 27 mile stretch of mathematically straight track, he searched the slightly elevated shelf above the nearby expanse of fresh blue water for some distinquishing feature. But there was scarcely a grade in the great gray plain as it swung downward in vast undulations to meet the upward sweep of the lake. None, except for Chicago, "Chekaugou," named after "stinking onions" by a French Black in 1804 when he visited a Winnebago Indian trading post.

Quickly expanding on the approaching horizon, Chicago appeared to be a big town in low-relief. And, as of August 12,1939, the city's low relief applied to the historical as well as a physical view. Nothing very salient had yet happened to her, other than perhaps the achievement of a harmonized trade and industry operation symbolized in forty-eight trunklines representing 59% of American railway mileage.

Communicating with more than forty million people in the great basin of the Mississippi, the world's richest valley, it was not an overworked cliche that all roads led to Chicago, the world's largest railroad center.

Noticing a reddish haze grow across the western sky, Firpo was immediately struck by a mysterious suggestion that there was a teeming and dynamic energy underneath.

Swiftly wheeling past pleasant suburbs with inviting stretches of green lawns and flowered homes, the young man soon lost the smoke-cloud because he had now penetrated it. Reeling miles of the backs of rotting flats passed by and he knew he was in Chicago's forsaken region which the metropolis had leaped over in growth. Here were the

Tony Firpo in August of 1939. An Italian-American born in Stockton, California, Tony was the nephew of Luis Firpo, Argentina's "Wild Bull of the Pampas," a prizefighter who at one point knocked Jack Dempsey out a ring.

grimy factories and old warehouses, the massive cattle yards and slaughterhouses, the freight depots and smaller terminals. Endless rows of miserable frame shanties in all stages of dilapidation abounded. Slowly reducing speed, the train cut through the corridors of crumbling old brick tenements with laundry hanging on the fire excapes, past the windows of people living so close to the tracks you could identify the flowers growing in their window pots. And, all along the route, Firpo saw slum children playing, often no more than a few feet from the tracks.

As he caught glimpses of such structures as the Wainwright Building, the Masonic Temple, and the Auditorium Tower, he reflected that in reality Chicago was nothing more than a series of cases of residence and trade in a desert of poverty, slaughter, and shipping.

Rumbling through narrow clefts of wooden tenements decaying in the sun, the passenger train suddenly plunged into a tunnel whose length seemed interminable. Then, just as suddenly, Firpo found himself gliding from its closed walls into open and vast railroad yards.

The train thread its way through the freight classification yards and a tangle of stock and flatbed cars, Pullman sleepers, mill-type gondola and 16,000 gallon tank cars, and hundreds of fan-equipped refrigerator cars. After passing turntables and engine houses, ice manufacturing plants and docks, shop facilities for the servicing and overhauling of locomotives and warehouses for their supplies and materials, the passenger train emerged into a single massive yard of black and gray passenger coaches. Almost crawling now, she selected a single pair of empty tracks between parallel covered platforms and groaned to a stop in the LaSalle Street Passenger Terminal.

Quickly emerging from the coach with his single straw suitcase, Firpo immediately felt the impact of a city prostrated by a humid heat. Feeling the sweat beginning to ooze out of him, he walked along a crowded high-level island platform to the main terminal. Asking a conductor for the Southern Pacific platform and the City of San Francisco connection to California, he mounted a gentle ramp and entered the labyrinth of Chicago's main terminal. Forested thickly with massive fluted columns against paneled backgrounds of glass and roofed solidly with laced concrete and steel, the lobby was the most impressive enclosed area he had ever seen.

Since he had an hour's wait, he decided to walk around the city. Crossing the high starryroofed concourse into the exit corridors lined with the terminal's toilets, baggage and mail rooms, news counters, fruit stands, drug stores, clothing shops, book, jewelry, and souvenir stores, barber shops and beauty parlors, a dry-cleaning establishment, restaurants, a bus terminal, and other small concessions, Firpo emerged into the hot morning sunlight. All around him were streets and pavements alive with a hurrying humanity drenched in sweat. An elevated subway train roared over head. Trucks and taxis clattered along the uneven granite streets. The gongs of buses and streetcars rang frantically, even though the countless vehicles seemed stationary. People by the thousands crowded the scorching pavements on their way to work, jostling, half-walking, half-running. Perspiring passengers on trapped buses and streetcars appeared unhappy. Someone nearby exclaimed he wished it would rain. Another commented that such an extreme heat was extraordinary for Chicago already legendary for her humidity. And, added to the humid, suffocating heat, Firpo noticed a haze of soft coal smoke drifting down, forcing people here and there to cough.

The central business section was bounded by the Chicago River on the north and west, the lake on the east, and Twelfth Street on the south. Shouldered next to each other were commercial buildings of every architectural period, a throwback to the eclecticism of the World Fair of 1893. A few structures flung themselves above the mass, but hardly enough to relieve the monotony.

Loose and cool in a white silk shirt and light summer seersucker pants, Firpo sauntered down LaSalle Street in the heart of the financial district. Crossing Randolph and State Streets, he passed the grand old movie palaces in their Moorish architecture. Great, fat buildings squatted everywhere sizzling in the burning morning sun. The mammoth Marshall Field department store still dominated this section of town. And, there was not a sprig of green anywhere. As he looked

Tony Firpo lettered in football at the University of California. A gifted athlete, he was ranked as one of the nation's finest tennis players.

around, he felt he would give half the price of all the congested architecture for the relief of a small green park. Duncolored structures, sad and be-smoked, shouldered grimly next to each other in a thick air buzzing with flies. A large cigarette sign had a man blowing smoke-rings around an inter-section, adding to the grotesqueness. Gazing up-ward, Firpo saw big, soot-incrusted and lifeless cubes in whose dark windows and corridors small lights faintly glimmered. As in a cave of doom, he reflected. And, eerily, there were great, buzzing crowds everywhere.

So this was the famous Loop, he thought, that part of the central city which has 2 tracks looping overhead. How ironic that all the streets nearby were named Elm, Cedar, and Oak and not a one of them could boast a single tree.

Turning back toward the terminal, Firpo felt the light, eternal cloud of smoke descend upon him. Once again he sensed something vastly energetic, although it certainly was not something beautiful.

Considered a major milestone in railroad prog-ress, the LaSalle Street Passenger Terminal cov-ered an area of 54 acres, much of it below street level similar to the Grand Central Station in New York. Entirely enclosed, the 600 trains which daily entered were never seen by people on the streets. Occasionally, a pedestrian would hear faint sub-terranean rumblings as trains entered the termi-nal approaches from the yards or far below the surface of the street.

The main structure was designed in austere Gothic, nearly 800 feet long, and 400 feet wide. Inside, the main concourse, one of the most im-pressive rooms in the world, had a height of 165 feet. Its floor space could accommodate 30,000 per-sons. Two years previously, on December 21, 1937, 252,288 passengers were handled in one 24 hour holiday rush period establishing a new American record. Known as the "Gateway To A Continent," the terminal and the yards were the most valuable piece of property in Chicago. Their assessed valua-tion was $36,000,000, a million and a half more than the assessment of the Empire State Building in New York.

The main terminal had two levels. The upper level, which connected with the main concourse, was largely used by long distance and transconti-nental trains while commuters and suburban trains arrived and departed on the lower level. The station's operating heart was a signal tower four stories high located above the yards. Here were located all the safety and signalling devices, elec-tropneumatic interlocking blocks, position light signals, teleautographs and train directors' tables, remote control power panels and coded continuous cab signals, and other apparatus for the efficient acceleration of traffic. From this tower, the Chief

Train Director planned all the terminal's opera-tions and train movements, giving verbal orders to each of the five levermen who set up the routes through the intricate system of switches.

Indeed, within the 54 acres, America had the most sophisticated communication and transpor-tation center for receiving and dispatching of goods and passengers that the world has ever known. To perform the functions of gate, storehouse, market, and point of shipment, three major belt railways coordinated the forty-eight other trunk lines. Lake steamers loaded and dis-charged goods at nearby docks which were quickly brought to the terminal. A unique transcontinen-tal institution known as the Office of the Railway Clearing Yards governed and amplified all the existing facilities for safe and secure interchange.

Firpo stopped before the impressive entrance. Showing a familiar and massive terminal clock above the classic portals by which countless thousands of travelers had set their watches, the station entrance was indeed alive. All around him perspiring people were coming and going. Com-muters hurried to work, not glancing one way or another. Tourists, however, emerging from all parts of America, filed past him slowly and hesitat-ingly. Dressed in disastrous hot-weather bulging shorts, over-weight mothers tugged at shrieking children who for some incomprehensible reason wore socks. Fathers in Hawaiian shirts carried overstuffed bags, smelling of everything from dirty underwear to bolony. Squalls of childish fury and murmurs of parental appeasement forced Firpo to smile. And amid the heat, mommas and poppas were gazing about the skyline with emo-tions of the deepest reverence.

Firpo crossed through the terminal entrance and stood for a few moments on the main concourse watching the crowded, almost festive like scene. He was amazed. Train gates to the right, ticket windows to the left, and three information booths situated in strategic settings. Huge electric fans were buzzing in every available corner in order to relieve the suffocating humidity. Further down the line, travelers bound for all points on the compass patiently waited for train platform gates to open.

Slowly treading his way between the crowds across the main lobby, Firpo noticed simple Traver-tine wall faces, Tennessee marble floors, and cof-fered ceilings. Having been an art minor in college, he felt that the most striking feature of the termi-nal's aesthetics was the dominating use of red in the ceiling contrasted with the bronze fixtures and paint in the ironwork decorations. Ten 18-foot long prismoidal lighting fixtures in bronze and translu-cent glass which were suspended from the ceiling in two longitundinal rows accentuated the over-all design. Walking up a long wide ramp to a mez-

Red caps handling baggage on the City of San Francisco in Chicago.

zanine level, he paused and looked down on the crowds.

Leaning over a terraced balcony above one of the main open-faced type bronze-grilled ticket-information counters, he decided to eavesdrop on the various conversations below. The ticket agent had a portable electric fan on the marble-top in front of him.

The job behind an information desk in a railway terminal must be wearing, Firpo thought. But then one meets such interesting and charming people. People standing in a long line to purchase tickets were fanning themselves as their shirts and dresses clung to their backs. Here and there men wore handkerchiefs wrapped around their necks to catch the sweat. People seemed weary, snappish, and exhausted, although it was only 9:30 a.m. For a second, Firpo reflected how defenseless people are before such an intense and unnatural heat. It was already too hot to move, let alone stand in line.

Down below a young woman in purple, clinging to a large suitcase, was angrily asking to purchase a ticket to California, specifying that she would ride on nothing but the City of San Francisco streamliner. The agent explained that the best he could do would be to place her on a waiting list.

"Waiting list! But the streamliner leaves in a few minutes! How long must I wait?" she exclaimed, her face puffing.

"Well, in most cases, you'd have to wait a full month, probably six weeks. But if there are any last minute cancellations, I'll let you know. You'd better stay close by."

"Please do what you can. Please! I must be on the coast next week, and I carry so much baggage that I must go by railroad, and if possible on the air-conditioned streamliner. Do you have other coast-bound trains that leave today?"

"Certainly. I can sell you a ticket for a passenger train that leaves in a few hours. That will get you there in 2½ days. But that's the ordinary way. If I can, I'll get you a seat and bunk on the streamliner. Space on it was sold from a month in advance."

"Why?"

"Because the public has gone streamline-minded in a big way. Travelers will take nothing less if they have any possible chance to ride the City."

"Well, please do what you can. I'd give anything to get whatever thrill there is in traveling on one of those snappy, stainless steel babies!"

The young woman moved off and waited patiently a few feet from the counter.

Next, a plump and anxious woman asked about the train for Brookfield Junction.

"Lady, you've been back three times! Yes, it will be all right to stop over night at Bethel."

"But are you sure, ticket-man?" she asked, "Are you sure? Do you really know it for a fact?"

A dressy young man, sweat pouring from his pale face, elbowed the anxious woman aside and purchased two weekend roundtrip tickets to Beverly Shores, Indiana. A blushing young woman with perspiration running down her temples catching in her mascara stood a few feet away watching him.

"Dressed the part to the limit, too," Firpo mused.

From all around, snatches of conversations floated upward.

A young woman announced icily to a fellow who had come to pick her up, "I've only been waiting thirty-five minutes, dearie!"

An anxious teacher walked up to two boarding school girls who were waiting by the information booth and exclaimed, "Ethel, your momma is waiting at the railway freight terminal on the other side of town. I don't know how she could have gotten mixed up. And, Dorothy, it seems your momma is meeting the wrong train on platform 5 though she's in the right direction, at least."

Firpo laughed softly. Then, he noticed a lovely young woman with heaving breasts admonishing a red cap to wait right there for her and guard her things while she powdered her nose. The porter seemed uncomfortable standing all alone guarding 12 pieces of luggage of every imaginable shape and color.

Nearby was a stern-looking elderly woman standing beside six canvas suitcases. When an old gentleman appeared and mumbled something, she raised her voice, "Why, Mr. Fowler, you never said the waiting room! You said the information desk as plain as plain can be!"

Firpo chuckled out loud when a sexy woman walked past the desk causing the ticket-information wizard to look up and stare, although he was right in the middle of a sentence to an old fellow who was determined to travel to Montreal and Quebec by way of Niagara Falls, Providence, and Brockton.

The front end of the streamliner shortly after it was dieselized in 1939.

And so it went. Perspiration beaded upon brows, armpits damp and obviously sticky, men and women obviously miserable. The scene was one of continuous fluttering of fans and folded newspapers.

With his hour layover nearly up, Firpo turned and sauntered toward Platform 19 where the Southern Pacific crack flyer would soon pull in for boarding. With one last glance over his shoulder, he reflected, "The booth labeled 'ticket-information' is not the place where people go to buy tickets and have their questions answered. Instead, its biggest clientele comes from those who think that it would be easier to meet there than at the taxi stand, waiting lounge, or out in front. What fun!"

★ ★ ★

The yardful of locomotives and sleeper trains lay for the most part silent, except for the sputtering of an uncertain safety-valve or the occasional clanging of a bell as an engine moved drowsily to a waterplug or coal-chute in the hot morning sun. Gangs of greasy wipers were already at work polishing cross-heads and side-rods of selected engines. A big H18 stood over an ashpit while a grimy yard man crawled between her drivers and banged and poked away at her ash-pans, amid clouds of

Ed Hecox stands in front of the City of San Francisco. A veteran engineer, he had secured the most prized position in the Southern Pacific Company. At the time of the derailment, he ran and stumbled along the track for over a mile in order to spread the alarm. After phoning for help, he returned to the tragedy in order to help direct emergency relief work.

steam and hot cinders. Although it was only 9:35 a.m., the temperature hovered above the 95° mark throughout the shed-covered service buildings and multiple-track approaches of the terminal yards. It promised to be Chicago's hottest day of the year.

Drenched in sweat, Engineer Ed Hecox casually strolled down the line of freights and engines, a few purring contentedly. Walking past a set of special tracks which had been raised 12 inches to allow easy inspection of full length trains and across a deep pit to facilitate removal of wheels and other heavy equipment that could not be repaired in place, Hecox caught a glimpse of the brilliant brown and orange colors against the silver background of the City of San Francisco.

As Hecox spotted Windy, his fireman, crouching behind a connecting rod probing a link motion with a long nosed oil-can, the entire scene seemed to be in soft focus as clouds of steam from various cleaning devices floated upward and around him and the streamliner. Hecox had been an engineer for over two decades and his haggard face gave vivid testimony to his reputation as a hard-working, conscientious man. He smiled at his fireman.

Windy was proud of the fact that he had been the first to drive eleven Pullmans 96 miles in an hour and a half back in 1910. Perspiration beaded upon his brow and shirt clinging to his back, the fireman was only a month away from retirement.

"Climb up," he said, grinning at Hecox. "We'll be on our way in short order!"

Looking at his watch, the fireman climbed out from behind the wheels and walked over to a long tank outside a nearby roundhouse and began washing off his greasy hands. Hecox climbed aboard, lit his pipe, and studied the allowance chart of oil for the run. A safety-valve sputtered and then popped with a roar as a small old man with a ragged jumper and a dirty golf-cap walked into the cab from the second power unit.

"Hello, Daddy!" shouted Hecox. "How's tricks?"

Daddy waved a jet-black hand. No one would have guessed that he was one of the oldest engineers on the road.

"This old junk'll be going to the shops before long," the old man shouted with a smile. "Can't get steam enough now to blow your hat off!"

"Oh, come off!" laughed Hecox, as he placed the clipboard back on the cab desk. "You know this coffee pot embodies the newest ideas of streamlined structural engineering. No expense has been spared to make the run into Frisco the strongest, safest, most comfortable, and smoothest ride ever built."

"You can't draw twenty-eight extra miles on this piece of junk like we used to fire every night on the old Trilby around the Loop. Old 8000, sure enough, was better than this hunk of scrap. Now, there was an acquaintance, old 8000. She did not look like the tail-truck comet of a mile-a-minute pace. She was solemn as night, but she got the work done without fancy skin or gadgets. Nowadays, all you do is groom for a day's performance, then race across the sage and back!"

"Well," Hecox said, "she might not be the puffin' and wheezin' woodburning locomotive of your days, but she sure handles pretty. Precision performance is the thing that counts today. The truth is, Daddy, that you set 'em up in '04 and have never ridden one of ours."

Windy climbed into the cab, "Daddy, the yard foreman wants you to carry half a bucketful of rivets over to the turn-table at Engine 5."

"Tell you what," the old engineer said as he backed down the ladder. "Railroading is a thankless job. Bad work, bad weather, and bad hours. If I were a young man again, I'd never go near a locomotive. There was a time when one man was a little better'n another, and the good man got the good engine and the good job and kept 'em both. Nowadays, a man is just a little interchangeable piece of machine, works when and where they tell him to, and sleeps when he gets a chance. No credit

Fireman "Windy" Kelly at the throttle of the City of San Francisco in July, 1939.

for what he does right, but the minute he slips up a little the office hollers, 'Thirty day!' or something. That's the kind of thanks you get!"

"So long, fast-freight artist!" waved Hecox, as he watched the old man amble between a line of simmering, groaning locomotives.

"That old guy is a peach," commented the fireman. "Everybody likes him and his complaining. He looks like a hobo, doesn't he? But the company keeps him on even though he's 74 now. He's always working around at some odd job like that. Other day some of the fellers sent over a bundle of overalls for him, but he won't wear them. Says they're too modern. They addressed it, 'For Daddy, the man that digs cellars daytimes and runs Trilby's at nights.' And the old guy hasn't a watch either. Used to pound the joints by star sighting, too."

Hecox chuckled and placed Windy's oil can in a cupboard. Then he looked out the cab window down the line. "Looks like we're all finished cleaning up," he remarked as he noticed the maintenance crews reassembling their hoses and washing out their buckets.

"Well, let's be moving her into place for boarding. Have to take the Y now, while Daddy is off somewhere else."

Hecox shoved the pipe into his mouth, again glanced out of the window, and released the automatic brake valve handle. By releasing the throttle in the diesel electric, the engines powered by oil fuel ignited by the heat of compression turned the generator which produced the electricity. A control unit sent the electricity to the axle-mounted traction motors which then turned the

31

The main control panel of the City of San Francisco.

wheels. Windy gave the bell-rope a pull, and soon, with the streamliner's connecting-rods beginning to clank and her seventy-six inch drivers slowly banging over the rattling switches, the City of San Francisco eased through the lines of locomotives, freight trains, and sleepers. As they passed other engines, Hecox and Windy shouted and waved to the cabmen. They in turn shouted something back and grinned. In a few minutes, they were on the connecting and adjacent tracks at a right angle to the main paralleling tracks leading into the terminal. Other passenger trains were moving out of the station in the opposite direction in accordance with specific rules and timetables.

With a groan of the independent valve brake-shoe handle, the streamliner stopped just beyond a switch, guarded by a dwarf signal.

"All right," shouted Windy as he gave the bell-rope another long pull. Hecox leaned out of the cab window, shoved the selector handle into the reverse position, and the City of San Francisco slowly began rattling back into the main passenger terminal for boarding.

★   ★   ★

People were gathered on the main departure platform well in advance of the 9:55 a.m. boarding time. Thousands of passengers enroute to other destinations also gathered on the through track layout directly adjacent to the main terminal. Nearby, red caps were busy trucking baggage and mail along the ten platforms coupled in pairs. Although protected from the sun by steel-framed canopies, people were nonetheless exhausted by the humidity.

Everyone on Platform 19 was expectant and excited. With all the noise and color, the scene was impossible to resist. Some individual passengers and families flecked with light touches of holiday spirit had brought picnic baskets filled to the brim. Children oblivious to the heat romped in glee along the platform while parents darted with cameras for photographic positions when the streamliner arrived. Firpo wandered through the crowd and decided to wait near the platform master's office.

A few yards away, a wrinkle-faced man set up a small stand and began selling tin replicas of the City of San Francisco.

"All aboard, boys and girls!" he shouted. "It's super speedy time for $1.29. You can buy an exact replica of the famed streamliner which whizzes under its own power. Made of sturdy tin, it is over 16 inches long and it runs anywhere without tracks for a length of 40 feet. Can't hurt mom's floor. Just wind the key and jeepers! It's off! Like the supersonic streak you'll be riding to California in just a few minutes! Hey, kids, be engineers of tomorrow!"

Just then, the beautiful young woman Firpo observed going off to powder her nose emerged from the main station level on an escalator and onto the crosswalk connecting all the platforms. The red cap dutifully followed behind her carrying all her bundles of luggage and handbags. Hotel pasters on her luggage indicated that she had been a toursit in various eastern American cities.

"First class passengers up forward for the City of San Francisco!" shouted a conductor to the people wilting in the heat as he passed down the 1,500 foot long platform. Spotting the young woman as he looked around hesitatingly, the conductor politely inquired, "Going through to San Francisco?"

"Oh, yes. They told me the streamliner would depart at 9:55 a.m. She hasn't arrived for boarding yet, has she?"

"Plenty of time before she departs," he smiled, touching his cap. "The porter will carry your luggage right onto the train and into your compartment."

"Lead off, sir!" she playfully ordered the red cap. "I'm game. I'm spending the last week of my vacation on that streamliner."

Down the congested platforms and beyond the domain of the double-tracks, the trim and graceful City of San Francisco could now be seen inching her way into the platforms. A flurry of exclamations went up among the crowd. People began to clap politely, whistle softly, and sigh. Stainless steel, duralumin, and Corten (metal alloys fighting for supremacy among themselves) formed the luster of her natural metal finish exterior.

As she slowly backed into her designated boarding place, Firpo was overwhelmed by her beauty. It was a moment he would never forget. She looked light, airy, and cool.

As the streamliner eased to a halt, an attractive young train stewardess in a chic blue-grey uniform and overseas cap appeared from within and held open one of the doors, calling out, "Step right aboard! Step right aboard, ladies and gentlemen!" All up and down the platform, passengers feverishly clambered aboard and flowed into the coaches.

Climbing aboard with the other passengers, Firpo found a window seat mid-way down a long row of plush-covered seats that bounded both sides of a wide aisle. He stowed his small suitcase in the open space under his seat. A huge woman, dripping with sweat, sat down in an adjacent seat across the aisle and began tearing into a salami and a hunk of cheddar. She smiled at him and exclaimed, "Looks like it's going to be an exciting trip!" Firpo sighed. Even though the modern streamliner would be in Oakland in less than 48 hours, it promised to be a very, very long trip, indeed.

A stewardess-nurse is working her way through the chair cars looking after the comfort of passengers, particularly women traveling with small children.

In the next coach stood Thelma Ristvedt, the stewardess-nurse. Smilingly, she welcomed passengers aboard while they filed past her looking for their reservation seats. In this first brief contact with all the varied types of passengers, Miss Ristveldt was subtly establishing a confidence, or a bond of human understanding, by graciously making them feel at home. Indeed, she was genuinely glad to be of service.

Thelma was one of several registered graduate nurses acting as stewardesses on various Southern Pacific streamliners. Collectively, the young women represented a development in the human side of railroading, "as spectacular as streamlining on the technical side."

With most of the passengers on board, the young woman casually walked to the coach at the head end reserved exclusively for women and young children. This first walk through the train was her "get acquainted" tour. Accompanying the conduc-

tor as he took up tickets, she introduced herself to each passenger, offering to be of assistance whenever needed, and making a note of each passenger's name. In so doing, she mapped out the major part of her work for the entire trip.

A mother with a baby or youngster meant that a special formula might have to be prepared and that the child would need baby-sitting while the mother went to dinner. A few seats beyond, a middle aged lady was concerned with whether or not she would be able to have certain foods required for her diet. Miss Ristvedt promised to arrange the matter with the dining car steward. Because a sixteen year old boy was enthralled by the romance of the streamliner and asked permission to visit the engine room, the stewardess offered to take him on a close-up look of the diesels during the first major stop out of Chicago. In the sleeping car, an elderly lady crippled with arthritis was offered assistance in undressing and dressing and

was asked whether she would like her meals served in her section.

Thelma actually made her job as she walked along. The result was an incredible work sheet of various schedules for babies' feedings, taking care of children, helping invalids and the aged, and schedules for performing a dozen other helpful services. And sandwiched into this worksheet were her six daily routine inspections of all the train's dressing rooms. Thus, she had no fixed book of instructions. Her dealings were with individuals and she had been chosen for her job out of hundreds of applications chiefly because of her ready adaptability and sympathetic understanding of the unpredictable needs of human beings.

Thelma had to be alert and clear headed in the face of emergencies. Not only had she to be a mother to the children she cared for, but she also had to be a capable dietician. The stewardess had to be able to give emergency treatment in case of illness, or until a doctor could be obtained. She had to be a cheerful companion to the lonely as well as a complete, walking information bureau on train schedules and operations. Thelma not only had to be a guide pointing out interesting scenic points of interest, but she also had to coordinate her activities with those of the conductor, brakeman, steward, waiters, porter, and station passenger agent. Because of this, her work was hard. Starting at 6:30 a.m., she continued nonstop until 10:30 p.m. or even later when emergencies arose. Between Chicago and San Francisco, she would walk over 11 miles, making 30 to 50 round trips through the train, opening and closing car doors some 1500 times.

During the trip she would be doing everything from shaving a paralyzed man to parading a group of youngsters through the train in order to give parents a welcome 30 minutes relaxation. In short, the stewardess had to be a friend to every single passenger.

Southern Pacific felt that Thelma, and others like her, were the first line of the company's public relations, as well as its most effective sales person.

In Miss Ristvedt's case, she brought a special warmth and enjoyment to the hundreds of passengers she encountered on each trip.

★ ★ ★

Soon, Firpo heard the sounds of doors clicking shut, and spotted a conductor hurriedly walking down the platform. Firpo glanced at his watch. 10:02 a.m., seven minutes behind schedule.

In the super-domed engine, Hecox read the position-light signals which gave their indications by the position of a row of three lights rather than by colors of traffic on his tracks. Windy checked the

In the lounge.

continuous cab signal so that he would know the condition of the block ahead of the train even between wayside signals.

Hecox quickly scanned the summary report from the Motive Power Department manager which described the inspection and maintenance from the previous week's 4,512 mile round trip between Chicago and Oakland. Reading quietly, Hecox went down the report:

"First, the front end of the train was placed over the inspection pit and underneath inspection made, the pit being long enough to accommodate approximately one-half of the train. When this was completed, the train was pulled forward and test made of the automatic train control equipment at the same time Diesel men were making tests of individual cylinders to determine the condition of pistons, valves, injectors, etc. Meanwhile, inspection of underneath equipment of the rear portion of the train was made and the car cleaners washed the exterior of the power cars. Underneath inspection consisted of pipefitters going under the train and running steam through the train line, checking all steam traps. Also, carmen inspected brake rigging, trucks, wheels and underframe."

Glancing at his valve winds and pressure gauges, Hecox noticed occasional movements of the allerons and made a few minor adjustments of his controls. The form-meter for blowing out dirty water from the boilers was normal and the steam grate shaker was in the ready position. Hecox looked out his cab window and down the line to the nearly empty platform. A few friends and relatives were waving to those who had boarded. The conductor sang out one last "All aboard!", then turned and gave Hecox the highball signal.

Looking ahead to the tracks fanning out in all directions, as well as the tracks spreading upward on a three percent grade to an upper level, Hecox released the throttle and pressed his foot on the dead man's pedal. The City of San Francisco began to inch forward.

The slight and gentle rolling sensation told Firpo that the train was at last in motion. The soft droning of an electric motor rising to a higher and higher pitch, and the now regular clickety-click of car wheels over rail joints were the sounds that came to his ears, helping to drown out the fragments of conversations in the coach.

Past stock pens with their feeding and watering facilities and past incoming suburban passenger trains, the streamliner slowly gained momentum. Slicing under several signal bridges blinking all their light signals and across a bridge spanning the Chicago River, the train was indeed offering a smooth, gliding ride.

Firpo drew a long breath and leaned back exhausted, eyes lightly closed. His smooth, handsome features bore the look of a champion athlete, one of America's top 12 tennis players. He again opened his eyes and watched the Chicago suburbs roll by. Traveling in the most modern air-conditioned streamliner ever made was really going to be a joy after long days of strenuous activity and long nights of anxiety.

Having been eliminated in the quarterfinals of the U.S. Open Tennis Tournament at Forest Hills, he was exhausted after 11 days of competition. Now, with only 39 more hours to go, he would be home. The cool refreshing sea of fog blowing in through the Golden Gate which generally blanketed the Bay Area during this time of year would be a welcome relief from the humid heat of the east.

Traveling by streamliner was the safest form of transportation, he reflected. Not only was it something you could take for granted, but it was the only way to travel. Now, after the poisonous air of Chicago and the hot, foul air of the terminal, he felt a relief lift from his mind.

The reddish orange glow of the metropolis had faded into a deep blue Illinois sky dotted with white cotton fluffs. The landscape was a patchwork of greens, browns, and greys. It was like watching an endless motion picture. The steady muffled roar of the engines and the rhythmic click of the

streamliner cruising over solid tracks were reassuring sounds.

Closing his eyes, Firpo soon was lost in a series of images. Flashing before him were scenes of his recent victories, his one major defeat (it wasn't even a close match), the fans and crowds, the wheeler-dealers and hucksters all interwoven in the sacred atmosphere of the nation's premier tennis event. As usual, Forest Hills was a wild carnival in an elitist sanctuary, but he loved every second of it. Dozing off, Firpo slept for several hours.

★　★　★

When he awoke, the streamliner was gliding along at a fast clip. Meadows, densely wooded slopes, and streams melted into a landscape of gentle rural beauty. Hopfields, orchards, cornfields, and green pastures in this part of the Missouri mid-west told Firpo, who was the son of a farmer, that the soil was indeed rich. Every few seconds a small town or village would fly by like a phantom. On a curve, the streamliner did not lurch in the slightest degree compared with the ancient passenger train he had taken from New York to Chicago. Catching the tilt of each curve, the City of San Francisco rounded it with no more disturbance than an increased roar of the wheels.

Firpo stood up and stretched. All around him people were chatting or reading newspapers, and each seemed unaware of the streamliner's hum now reaching a shrill soprano pitch as it gained more and more speed.

Walking to the end of the aisle, he peered into the opposite compartment also filled with lounging passengers. Outside, factories of light industry began melting into sparsely settled suburbs and the streamliner seemed to be swooping down from a position in mid-air. The clickety-click of the wheels on the rails were now beating with the rhythm of a fast gallop played by an orchestra.

"A wonderful train!" remarked a well-dressed man who sat opposite observing Firpo's fascination.

"Yes, it does very well!" he smiled. But Firpo was really in no mood for conversation. Almost spellbound, he wanted to watch the scenery streak by at 75 miles per hour. Fertile farms, country houses, streams, orchards, and cattle — all seemed as if they were bewitched.

"I've never traveled so fast," Firpo said as he turned to the friendly gentleman.

"And what better way to see America? To boot, there is no better way to meet Americans from all walks of life, people as diverse as the regions from which they come," the man smiled.

Firpo agreed, and headed for lunch in the diner.

Meal time on the streamliner found the diner and coffee shop crew faced with a huge task. On such a journey over 200 meals would have to be served in the diner three times a day, while the popular coofee shop would handle another 300 servings or snacks.

As Firpo entered the car, he noticed tavern car attendants pursue their duties with a pleasantness where friendliness and congeniality had to be paramount. The head steward, whose main responsibility was to see that the dining car crew functioned smoothly and efficiently, walked forward and beckoned Firpo to sit at an unoccupied table.

As he sat down and glanced around, he thought to himself that one of the nicest aspects of train riding was that people loosen up and talk to each other as they rarely do in other forms of cross-country transportation.

At the table across from him, a railroad buff was talking at great length to an older couple about the economics of railroading:

"During the depression, railroad passenger revenues dropped 50%. Only the generous aid from the government saved some of the big boys from bankruptcy. Last year, American railroads in general earned a total net profit of $155,000,000. No question about it, the shiny new streamliners will lead American transportation out of the wilderness. . ."

Services and facilities on board the City of San Francisco appealed to women travelling with children. They had exclusive use of a chair car and a stewardess-nurse who was on call 24 hours a day to help mothers.

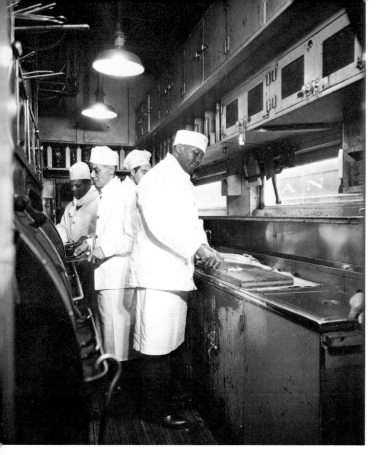

Chefs preparing meals in the ultra-modern kitchen.

The fellow was on his way to visit his mother in Berkeley and was the kind of man who was not used to having anyone interrupt his lectures. "Thank God he's not sitting at my table," thought Firpo. "This lecture might last a half hour."

At the table in front of him, three Black porters sat eating a hurried meal before the noonday meal rush began. Although the coach was fully air-conditioned at a comfortable temperature of 68°, all three men looked as if they had been sprayed with a garden hose.

Two of them were veteran train waiters and the third was evidently a cook. All agreed that the City of San Francisco was probably the best train in America and they were proud to have been assigned to her. Not only was the streamliner the newest and most modern the world has ever known, but it cut through some of the wealthiest cities of the mid-west picking up passengers who weren't afraid to lay out a dime for a tip.

"Shoot, just look around in a few minutes. On other trains, nobody buys food or drinks. They bring their own. By the time other people get to where they're going there are chicken bones all over the floor. Not here. Our people want nothing but gourmet, first class food. On other trains, you put mushrooms on top of steaks and hillbillies ask, 'What the hell's them thangs?' "

The white-haired cook nodded. "The railroad could make a fortune on other trains selling chicken and ham and hog chitlins, hog ears, and hog feet. Hillbillies coming on from Virginia would love it. Those folks know every part of a hog from his toes to his eyeballs."

Firpo smiled and gazed out the window while he waited to place his order. Palmyra Junction rolled into view, a sleepy little town surrounded by lush, gentle hills bathing in bright sunshine. The depot platform was almost empty except for two old men in rocking chairs and a few Black railroad workers who waved as the streamliner cruised past.

The young man ordered a bacon and cheese sandwich. Within moments it was served. Not only did it look delicious, but it was served ceremoniously. The long-term veteran waiter seemed to enforce certain rules with an almost arrogant zeal.

As Firpo sipped his coffee, a wind started blowing across the landscape and threatening clouds became darker. A sudden cloudburst was imminent, he thought. Soon people in the small towns the train sped through were scattering as the first drops made their appearance. At first the rain came down slowly and quietly. But within a few minutes it exploded upon the streamliner, not in individual drops, but like a waterfall accompanied by lightning that lit up the entire sky like a flare. The storm demanded that one listen and watch it and Firpo was riveted to it. Then, just as suddenly as it appeared, it vanished, leaving long streaks on the streamliner's windows and large puddles on the landscape.

With a sigh, he turned from the window. But he was suddenly startled to find the beautiful young woman he had observed in the station sitting quietly at his table smiling at him. He hadn't noticed her sit down.

"Oh, I'm sorry. I guess I didn't see you," he blushed.

"So I see. The rain was coming down so hard you didn't hear me. My name is Cristina. I'm a graduate nursing student in Chicago and I'm going to California on vacation."

Wearing a simple striped dress, she appeared to be about 5'6" and slim. Her head was tilted in such a way that her features were foreshortened and shadowed. Only her hair was caught by the shafts of sunlight pouring through the window.

Fingering his coffeecup, Firpo introduced himself.

"Really?", she exclaimed, "you were defeated by Don Budge?"

"Without much question to it, either. I probably played the best match of my life and still lost 6-2, 6-1. I could never expect to go beyond the quarterfinals. I'm on my way to coach tennis at the College of the Pacific in Stockton, California, near where I live."

"I'm training to be a neurobiologist," Cristina said after a pause. "To me, one of the most fascinating subjects for the scientist is the study of the human brain and human behavior. Neurobiological research, I hope, will lead to an understanding of the basis of emotional illness. I really would like to help relieve the anguish of psychologically disturbed people."

Firpo was impressed. He smiled and said nothing. A waiter took her order for lunch and Firpo asked for a second cup of coffee.

"Then you're coming to San Francisco?"

"Yes! After that, I'll spend a few days in Los Angeles before returning to the University of Chicago."

"San Francisco will delight you. As soon as you get off in Oakland and board the connecting ferry, or take the bus across the new Bay Bridge, you'll find all kinds of attractions."

"It's the different atmosphere of the West Coast I'd like to experience. In fact, if I like it I might move out and study at the University of California. It'll be a new taste of life for me during these next two weeks. Of course, I look forward to seeing those tiny, picturesque, almost funny crawling cable cars over the San Francisco hills."

The streamliner stretched out now at what seemed to be a breakneck speed. The landscape offered Firpo an exhilaration he rarely knew. Rivers wound their way languorously through small, weather-worn plains and valleys. He was indeed enjoying a freedom that no other form of travel allowed.

A huge woman with platinum hair and dressed in a bright purple suit sat down at the table and exclaimed, "95 degrees in Chicago wasn't fit for human habitation!"

Both Firpo and Cristina smiled at her, paid their bills by leaving money on the table, and walked out together.

★ ★ ★

Sitting in his elevated cab seat, Hecox again lit his pipe and settled down to watch the signals and switches fly by in rapid succession. Occasionally shifting his foot from the dead man's pedal and checking his load indicator, speed gauge, and fuel pump circuit breaker, the engineer was proud to be at the controls of the most powerful streamliner engine in the world.

There was just no question about it. The City of San Francisco boasted the most modern engineering concepts ever developed for a streamliner. And, Hecox, after nearly a half century of driving every imaginable pounder, was proud to have been assigned the most coveted position among Southern Pacific railroad men.

Now, with the streamliner "pounding the joints," as old timers called making speed, she boomed over bridges and swept through short tunnels, her engine sounding hollow and uncanny. Slowly, the engineer allowed the speed to increase until the speed indicator on the panel control box showed the streamliner averaging 83 m.p.h. Crashing over switches that sounded loose, and shooting through towns that were a confusion of buildings along the track, the City of San Francisco sailed along as if motionless.

"Like shooting the chutes, isn't it? Only fun we have on this run," shouted Windy. Through open fields and across hollow-sounding bridges, the streamliner roared on.

And, there was no question in anyone's mind that she was travelling at a perfectly safe speed.

★ ★ ★

Through the window of his roomette early the next monring, Firpo could barely make out drifting mists enveloping the Colorado landscape, a thousand gray wraiths crawling through the air, their thin bodies changing, contracting, vanishing. The sky was brightening, distant lights of purple and pink fighting their way through the mists, a dim burning of color like that of fire through smoke. As the streamliner plunged along, the vague shadows of the night were congealing into trees, rail fences, and farm buildings. Beyond them were more trees, stone walls, and red barns. From the earth rose the fresh odors of a new day.

Throughout the streamliner, travelers peered sleepily at the picturesque, checkered countryside.

In his compartment, the young man dressed and shaved. Since breakfast wouldn't be served for another half-hour, he decided to write a few letters to the new friends he had met at Forset Hills.

During the night the streamliner had stopped in Topeka. Now, the track was curving upward into southern Nebraska. Firpo could see the church spires in towns set in the midst of old red-brick structures. Passing through stations, crossing bridges and rivers, twisting through valleys and cutting into hills, here and there penetrating short tunnels, the luxury liner steamed along. Cruising alongside a river stream, he stopped writing to enjoy the turbulence of small rapids and boulders jutting from the waters.

★ ★ ★

Later that afternoon, Firpo and Cristina sat together back in the lounge car quietly sharing their thoughts. Behind them, they overheard a salesman in a double-knit leisure suit saying, "I've always been lured by the siren song of the train whistle. You see, I grew up near the tracks and as a boy every time a train would pass, I wished I were on it."

Firpo smiled at Cristina.

"Did you ever feel like that?"

"Yes, I must admit that I have. This trip represents a once-in-a-lifetime vacation for me. Besides, how could I resist such a streamliner with the bewitching name City of San Francisco?"

The young man turned his already tanned face to the sun streaming in through the broad windows. It felt so good. Closing his eyes, he lay back. The whole world had become serene.

Porters streamed by with drinks, making it harder and harder to pick up the sound of wheels on the rails over the tinkling of ice cubes.

And, in rapid succession, small towns like Glenwood Pines, Grand Valley, Cameo, Book Cliff, and Mack glided by.

★ ★ ★

There were many thoughts in Firpo's mind as he sat alone early that evening. The streamliner was plunging through the jogged, uninteresting scenery of western Colorado and eastern Utah. Dreary mesquite bushes, low mountains, red earth as far as the eye could see. Nothing moved but the wind and puffs of whitish dust. Even the striated clouds hung still against the warm sky. Now and then a blossoming red-flowered Palo Verde tree unfolded along the way and flickered like flames in the shadows of the descending sun. Here and there two or three tree lilies swaying gently could be seen taming the landscape. And up ahead, the endless twin bands of track iron shot across the desert depths over vast undulations of sagebrush slopes. As the streamliner passed a dry riverbed blooming with oleander, he spotted a small owl roosting on a huge stone. The landscape was gradually growing gentler. The alluvial valleys in the region showed they were formerly wide, shallow drainages. Here and there between deep, straight-banked arroyos were small towns brimming with orchards — the apricots glimmering like gold on the trees and hulking clusters of loquats showing through the dark thick leaves.

After an hour's stop in Salt Lake City to pick up more passengers, the streamliner cut through the southern portion of the lake. The salt sea stretched out to Firpo's right, appearing infinite, deep blue, and foamy. And all around were the outlines of mountains, the peaks of low hills smoldering in the day's last sun rays.

Beyond the Great Salt Lake, the entire landscape took on an unexpected sweetness. The thyme, daffodils, and poppies, all the familiar elements one encounters on a northern Italian mountainside were there. In the distance, Firpo even spotted a young shepherd with his sheep, goats, and dogs. Joshua trees, with their banana-like blooms on the ends of the branches offered him and his flock protection from the stinging sun.

★ ★ ★

The sun was finally setting, shadows lengthening and touching the desert. The sky soon began glittering, playing and twirling with the stars. A full moon was reflected on the flat, almost sparkling earth. It would be an excellent night for laying out the constellations of August, the young man thought, but he was still too numb with the exhaustion of too many things happening in too short a period of time.

Firpo sat back smiling, making no effort whatsoever at thought. He was tired, gently happy, and settled comfortably. The brittle metallic of the speeding streamliner was slowly putting him to sleep.

★ ★ ★

Two hours later, he awakened.

"The most sumptuous train of the decade," thought Firpo. "She really is luxury de luxe on rails speeding through Nevada."

A wheeled city all of her own, the streamliner was combining lightning-quick transportation with the ease and comfort of an ultra-modern hotel. Using the newer alloys, a knowledge of aerodynamics, articulation between units and new principles of construction, Southern Pacific was displaying its most effective weapon in transportation's new offensive for more and profitable passenger business. In her coaches, 165 passengers were idling away the 39 hours and 30 minutes between Chicago and San Francisco.

It was the night of August 12, 1939.

Looking out over the desert night, one couldn't help but reflect that it hadn't been long before when ox-drawn prairie wagons had crawled their way through the sage-brushed state. And, just a few years before, passenger trains took their time, ambling across the west with little concern as to when they reached their destinations. But not any longer. Now, 5400 horse power condensed into three diesel-electric giants of power pulled 17 cars over the same route at a speed of a mile a minute.

In the lounge cars, men and women sat sipping cocktails or chatting in careferee relaxation. A small group clustered around the bar. The club car with its indirect lighting was filled with other relaxing people lost in books and magazines. In the compartments and drawing rooms of the coaches, sociable groups spent the evening as they would at home, pausing occasionally to pick up the tele-

"Quality service at economy prices" boasted the Southern Pacific advertisements. The following interior photographs were taken in the club car Embarcadero one month before the derailment.

phone and order a snack from the diner. Even at this late hour, every chair in the barber shop was filled with patrons.

The outside night was sultry, but air-conditioning made the train's interior cool and comfortable. Even the usual stops and starts in Elko and Carlin were of little concern, since the streamliner had been designed to move like a single unit of rolling stock.

Nearing their California destination, everyone was happy. Some talked happily of reunions and noisy receptions, or of the loved ones who would be meeting them at the Oakland pier. Others carried vivid memories of farewells shouted in New York or in Chicago — the parting words of friends calling "pleasant journey."

And there were those passengers who already had scribbled messages they would wire back home upon their safe arrival in San Francisco. After all, with an amazing safety record through long years of service, railroad travel in America had been recognized and accepted by everyone. And in maintaining that record, Southern Pacific had been outstanding, a model for modern railroading the world over.

There was not one among the carefree travelers who sensed the nearness of death. Certainly, Hecox was not aware of impending disaster as he looked out his cab and saw stars forming behind the shadowy mountains and immense cliffs which lined the twisting valley of the Humboldt River.

As he sat on his comfortable seat with a foot on the deadman pedal and a hand near brakes which were tuned to the sensitive touch of his fingers, he nearly filled the window cab. With the confidence of an experienced railroadman, the 65-year-old veteran engineer leaned slightly forward keeping his eyes glued to the track ahead illuminated by the piercing headlights.

Hecox and Windy were aware of their responsibility. They knew that scores of human lives were in their hands. And, they also knew their train with all of her complicated safety features. Safely piloting the $2,000,000 rolling leviathan was something they could do with the ease of an elevator man.

The City of San Francisco, Southern Pacific's train No. 101, drew to a stop at Harney to pick up a lone passenger. Within seconds, the signal came to proceed and the streamliner glided off again, gaining speed as the little station faded away in the night. For a few seconds, the deep-throated rumble of the great diesels and the rhythmic clickety-click of the wheels on the rails were the only sounds heard in the Nevada desert.

Hecox glanced at his watch. It was 9:16 p.m.

"Twenty-eight minutes behind schedule," he remarked to Windy who was standing by his side.

"Nothing to worry about," replied the fireman. They both knew they would arrive in Oakland on time since there would be no further stops before Sacramento. During the night they could open the diesels up to full power, 90 m.p.h.

It was a beautiful moonlit night, and as the streamliner glided by the desert bogs outside Harney, Hecox could hear the frogs peeping above the gentle rumbling of the streamliner. As the chief veteran of the Southern Pacific lines, the engineer had guided the City of San Francisco since her maiden voyage seven months before.

Windy was quietly whistling as the streamline gained momentum.

At 9:33, Hecox looked at his watch again and noted that the pride of Southern Pacific's fleet of crack flyers was making 60 miles an hour as she quietly clicked along hitting the various mileposts to the second. He peered ahead and saw that they were approaching the curve leading to bridge no. 4 spanning the Humboldt River.

As the train moved smoothly along, he saw for a brief moment a tumbleweed, or Russian thistle, lying across the tracks in the glare of the headlights.

Suddenly, he felt his own car lurch and jump the tracks, then thud, thud, thud along the wooden ties across the bridge out of control. Death in all her possible violent agony began.

The huge streamliner trembled, rocked, and swayed as steel snarled on rocks and ties. For a split second there was a terrifying rumble similar to a distant earthquake as speeding coaches furiously leaped from the rail. There followed a horrifying roar, as if a thousand freight trains were colliding. Resounding over the flat, quiet desert, the roar turned into the screeching, splintering, slashing sounds of crunching steel, as if some fiendish giant were squeezing the train together with his mighty hands. Accompanying this sickening grinding of steel striking metal and rock, tracks being yanked from their ties, metal car walls made of the strongest steel being ripped open, folded and crushed, were the sounds of a people trapped in terror. Death could not have chosen a better spot to strike. Out of control, the streamliner's middle coaches snapped their connections with the engines and slammed into the old iron bridge. Cars telescoped into each other, steel crashing and crunching. A dining coach filled with late dinner passengers and retiring waiters and cooks was tossed like a toy replica into the air and landed in a jagged, twisted heap in the river, with a club car nosing down after it; two other cars followed, hurtling against the heavy steel girders of the bridge, while other coaches simply overturned.

A map of the derailment site indicating the tragedy occurred between Harney and Palisade in eastern Nevada.

The heavy, rusty steel girders of the bridge swayed, then snapped and collapsed like so much cheap tin into the stream below. Five more cars loaded with terrified, panic-stricken men and women toppled down on top of them. The beams of the bridge jutted in every possible angle, like so much matchwood. In the scrap pile of mashed hulls, the once beautiful City of San Francisco lay in the throes of agonized death.

In the Pullmans, many passengers had already retired for the night. As the streamliner plunged into the river, people were flung from their beds to the floor or against the walls. Others in the comfortable club car, the lounges, and the diner were hurled against each other like so much waste. The interiors were a maelstrom of flying dishes, personal belongings, baggage, and loose furniture.

Here and there the force of the impact threw luckless travelers through the coach's windows, or sent them plummeting to the bottom of an upturned, splintered coach standing on end in the shapeless wreckage.

The powerline of all the coaches snapped and all the lights went off. Pitch black of night added to the first moments of horror as panicked people trapped in the twisting, rolling mass struggled frantically for their lives.

The streamliner's cab and power units had somehow crossed the bridge and did not overturn while her coaches had buckled up and plunged into the river. When the engines stopped, Hecox jumped down from the cab. For a moment, he was in a daze. He heard nothing but a deadly silence, except for the sound of hissing and spinning

SOUTH

Point of Derailment

A panoramic view of the derailment site.

A U.S. army aerial view of the sabotage. This perspective is looking west.

Bell Ranch
Harney, Nev.
W. P. R.R.

wheels. Then the screams began, slowly at first, rising to great crescendoes. And strangely, there was laughter, too, a kind of hysterical laughter emerging from somewhere in the twisted pile of metal. Everywhere there was dust, huge clouds of dust settling on everything since there was no breeze or wind. From the dust emerged the piercing moans and screams of the injured and dying, of people frantically struggling to extricate themselves from among the dead and dying, wiggling free from any possible opening.

At first Hecox could not see a single living being because of the thick dust. Slowly, he began distinguishing people climbing to safety out of gaps in the walls, out of windows and doors. Most were in night clothes. Others had their garmets torn, blood running from cuts of all kinds. It was an indescribable scene. All that the engineer could think of was, "Thank God there is not fire."

Without a word to Windy who was standing stunned in the cab doorway gazing down upon the scene, Hecox started running down the track toward the lights of Harney's station a few miles away. As he fought his way along, the cries of the dying and suffering slowly grew dim. A few passengers from among the more fortunate who had worked their way easily out of the wreckage scurried after him for help.

Reaching the Harney Station ten minutes later, Hecox told the startled attendants that there had been a terrible derailment up ahead and to call for doctors, nurses, ambulances and bandages. Hecox asked one of the section crew to immediately place

a call to the Southern Pacific headquarters in San Francisco. Although bleeding from cuts and bruises sustained from running and stumbling along the tracks to Haney, he refused first aid and led the crew of four men back down the tracks toward the tragedy.

★ ★ ★

Forty miles away in Elko, telephones began ringing all over town. Every known doctor and nurse was being called for duty. During the next 30 minutes, six doctors and 20 nurses were recruited from the Elko Hospital and private nursing homes. Within an hour and 30 minutes, they boarded a special train loaded with supplies and were sped to the scene.

By midnight, an additional seven more doctors and eight nurses were rushed by special train from Reno. By 3:00 a.m., four more relief trains were dispatched from Ogden, Utah, and Sparks and Carlin, Nevada.

★ ★ ★

Although it was still early, Firpo had retired to his compartment bed on the left side of the car. Turning on his right side, he was dozing off. The rhythmic click of the wheels on the track seemed a bit faster than usual and he wasn't paying much attention to the speed of the streamliner. Nonetheless, the gentle rumble and swaying was soothing; and for him, it was a perfect way to fall asleep.

45

A general diagram view naming the cars in the pileup.

Suddenly, he felt the sensation of very rapid, violent bumps. Startled, he opened his eyes and raised himself up on his elbow. Outside it was dark. But he noticed large sparks flying past the window and in those few seconds the bumps became more and more violent. As he felt the sensation of air brakes being applied, the car started to tilt. Immediately the lights in the corridor went out. His suitcases stacked neatly above his bed tumbled out of their lockers striking him on the head and shoulders as he attempted to scramble up out of bed. Then the car tipped completely over. In an instant, the car seemed to be floating through space. It landed with a tremendous crash in the Humboldt River bed, right side up. At that moment, Firpo blacked out.

When he regained consciousness a few seconds later, he found himself sitting up on the compartment side, bleeding from a number of face and arm cuts and wounds. Strangely, he felt no pain. All around him was broken glass. Next to him was the open window. Reaching down, he could feel weeds and grass.

Everything was quiet. Then he heard the first screams and the sounds of people attempting to break through their windows. In an instant, he realized that a fire might break out and he scrambled to his feet. Dazed, he reached for the door. But the compartment door had broken completely off and he cut his legs scrambling over it. Now, in increasing pain, he groped along the corridor on his hands and knees until he reached the bar car which was immediately to the rear of his compartment. A number of passengers had already assembled in this car. Someone suggested they break a window in order to climb out. Firpo tore a piece of metal from a section of the bar table and used it to batter a window open. Although he was only in his shorts, he crawled through on top of the coach and immediately began hoisting out the passengers trapped inside. He lowered them to safety on the south bank of the river.

After rescuing eight, he went to work all along the overturned coach breaking windows from the outside. The night was quite dark and it was

Various angles of the pileup.

A closeup view of the west abutment with the Embarcadero in the foreground and the Presidio lying against the abutment in the upper right.

difficult to see. After aiding several others of the trapped out, he jumped down from the coach and assisted a number of men attempting to build bon fires on the tracks. From the light of these fires, he noticed that the lefthand rail was laying on its side. The righthand rail appeared to be in fair alignment and was right side up. The ties appeared to have been run over as though by huge wheel flanges. Their marks were just inside of the rail by about 2 inches.

Although his bleeding began to stop, Firpo was nonetheless in great pain. Yet, he ramined helping the injured as best he could. Now and then, there would come a call to help remove a passenger out of a trapped compartment and he would stumble over and assist. His thoughts returned time and again to Cristina but he could not leave the rescuing operations in order to look for her.

Finally, around 4:00 a.m., he boarded the makeshift relief train which had arrived, and was taken to the Elko General Hospital.

★ ★ ★

While Firpo was being bandaged in the Elko hospital, Cristina was giving her deposition as to what happened to a Southern Pacific agent:

"I was a passenger in the car Golden Gate which was either the fifth or sixth car from the rear. It came to a rest standing at an angle or slant and was sufficient to throw me out of my berth. Immediately, I assisted an elderly lady out of the upper berth above me into a lower berth on the opposite side which was the low side of the car and then I got out of the car as quickly as I could crawling to the front end on

48

The car Chinatown is resting on the overturned steel bridge, with the car Fisherman's Wharf on the left. The beams of the bridge have already been cut into sections by oxy-acetylene torch.

my hands and knees. I was assisted off the train, over the truck of this car, by several men on the outside. I could not say whether the truck was cut from underneath the body of the car or not, but I crawled out of an opening in the door stepping on to it. Then the men helped me to the ground. I saw the train and pullman conductors together and immediately went to them offering my services, since I am a graduate nurse. Following that, I got up onto the front platform of the car to the rear of the one in which I had been riding and put on the available clothing I had taken out of the car with me. After that the conductor called and wanted to know where the graduate nurse was.

The barber on the train had found the stewardess and assisted her, I think, out of the canyon, and we took her back to the observation car on the rear end of the train where we made her as comfortable as possible and I rendered what first aid I could. She urged me to leave her and go out to the others suffering and I spent the rest of the night between the stewardess and two women suffering from

shock whom we had made comfortable on pillows near the fire. I gave stimulants (procured from the club car) to these ladies and numerous others who were nervous and chilled. The ladies were placed on the ground near a fire made with railroad ties close to the east end of the canyon on the north side of the track and opposite the rear end of the car Golden Gate in which I had been riding. I was worried about my friend, Tony Firpo, but could not take the time to look for him. I prayed that he be safe.

The relief engine came about three a.m. and coupled itself to the cars on the rear of the train which hadn't been derailed. I do not know how many cars were attached as I was then with the stewardess in the observation car.

★ ★ ★

Ernest Betts, a husky young professor of teacher education at Pennsylvania State College, knew no medicine beyond first aid. Immediately after the crash, he walked through rows of injured passen-

A view of the demolished cars downstream from the bridge. A Southern Pacific employee is standing on the Mission Dolores. To his right are the cars Embarcadero and Twin Peaks. Chinatown is on the upper left.

Looking north from the river showing demolished bridge and the Presidio broken up on the west abutment. The Mission Dolores is in the left foreground with the Embarcadero to the right.

Looking downstream at the old bridge. It was simply known to Southern Pacific personnel and residents of the area as "Bridge, 4th crossing, Humboldt River."

This photograph is looking west across the bridge opening from the east abutment showing the demolished bridge in the river. The car Chinatown is resting on what remains of the bridge. The car Presidio is shown on the south wing of the west abutment.

gers and crew members in the intact coaches, applying tourniquets, binding wounds, and ripping his own clothes for bandages.

"This is going to hurt like hell, but hang on," he would say to someone hurt. "It will only hurt for a minute and then it will get numb."

Injured men and women smiled through the pain at the gruff words. And, they hung on while Betts ripped still another bandage from his shirt, or tightened a bit of cloth above a severed artery.

While attending to someone else's wounds, Betts would casually brush the blood out of his own cuts and scratches without bothering stopping to bandage them. He had left the fatal dining car of the train only a moment before it crashed. Somehow he had been thrown into the canyon with his clothes nearly torn off. Without shoes, he began wandering barefoot over the rough rocks of the river bank. But within moments while groping in the dark, he found a man bleeding to death. Kneeling, he started applying a tourniquet. Soon, there were others lining up for bandages.

Dr. Brigham, the only physician among the passengers.

Ernest Betts

And, behind him came Dr. F.G. Brigham, the only licensed physician among the passengers, replacing some of his bandages with more professional tourniquets and easing the pain of sufferers with morphine. Later, Brigham told officials:

"Mr. Betts was the real samaritan in the wilderness who all by himself saved the ebbing lives of at least 30 passengers. Probably more! He simply wouldn't let them die. Although not a medical doctor and although his system of hand bandages and tourniquets were crude as the niceties of medical practice go, he stopped the flow of blood long before dawn until I could get there. Some of the bandages I changed only to prevent gangrene from setting in."

With all his luggage lost, Betts later boarded a relief train in order to keep his Monday morning 9:00 a.m. appointment to address an education guidance clinic at Alameda High School in Oakland.

Edgar Metoyer

★ ★ ★

No one performed more herculean feats in pulling people from the wrecked streamliner in the river bed than Edgar Metoyer, a Southern Pacific porter.

From all sides came stories of Metoyer's heroic work: how he waded time and again into the water to carry some half-conscious person to safety; how he dived into the murky river to drag another survivor to shore.

Metoyer himself could not say how many people he saved. He was more willing to talk of the cold he contracted than the brave acts he performed.

"I was behind the bar in the observation car — last one on the train — when I felt the first hump. The blow knocked me against the wall and my head hit a shelf. Glass sprinkled all over. I guess I was knocked out. Then the barber on the train came and shook me to see if I was all right. We both shook ourselves and climbed out of the car to see what we could do. It was dead quiet outside — none of that screaming and shouting which came a few seconds later. We were on the wrong side of the train to get down where the people were, so we just climbed down the river bank and through the cars and started fetching them out.

When the barber on the train wasn't helping me carry people, someone else was. We just went in and out of the water until we got everyone there was. It sure was cold.

Tony Sherman — he was bartender in the club car — helped me for quite a while. He thought he was all right. But after a while he keeled over and the doctor said some of his ribs were broken. I walked by in the field by the fires once and there was Miss Ristvedt. She was groggy herself from a crack on the head, but she just went around helping other folks without tending to her own injuries.

I spent the rest of the night going back into the cars for blankets and mattresses and getting whisky for those the doctors said needed it.

I'm pretty tired now. But I sure hope this cold doesn't get bad."

★ ★ ★

The name of Thelma Ristvedt, 23, was that most often spoken as survivors recalled the harrowing night that followed the crash. She was the true heroine of the trying hours between the crash and the arrival of doctors and nurses early the next morning.

She had narrowly missed death in the crumpled dining car. Bleeding from head wounds and working solely on instinct and nerve, she fought her way out of the wrecked train to administer first aid to the injured, dragging others to safety and comforting those not seriously hurt.

Ironically, this had not been Thelma's regular run. She was just filling in a vacation schedule for another stewardess. Ordinarily she worked out of Omaha, although her permanent home was in Florence, South Dakota.

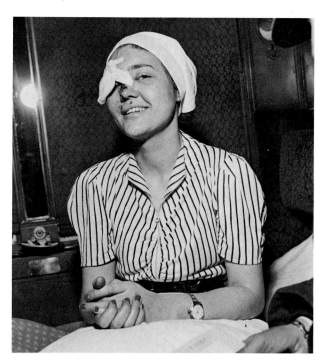

Thelma Ristvedt, the 23 year old stewardess-nurse, who saved countless lives until she was overcome by exhaustion and the loss of blood.

Just 60 seconds before the fatal crash, she left the dining car and walked into the club car in order to deliver some telegrams and make her final round of the train before retiring. She had taken only a few steps down the aisle when the train pitched and jammed the nose of her car into another coach.

The girl was thrown 30 feet by the impact, striking her head on a table. Half-blinded with blood, she stumbled to her feet to help the others in the car. There were seven persons there and only one was uninjured. The rest were badly hurt. Several were unconscious. Ristvedt started dragging them from the train. One by one she tugged the six injured persons to safety, carefully not aggravating their injuries. Outside she administered first aid with what little materials she had available.

Thelma, a fully trained stewardess nurse, helped everyone on her side of the stream. She even found sheets with which to cover the dead. Where she couldn't give aid herself, she directed others. Then Thelma tried to get to the others across the stream who might need her.

Nearly worn out, she waded into the icy waters and up the bank on the other side. There, weak from loss of blood and suffering from severe shock, she collapsed in utter exhaustion.

Doctors found her asleep on the river bank, her blond head pillowed on her arm and her ugly head wound still unattended. When a doctor bent over her to treat the wound, Thelma's eyes fluttered and she struggled to get up in order to go back to work. There was simply no quitting for her.

Every man and woman on the train saw her at one time or another, or heard of the good work she had done. She had not only been an inspiration to all the others, but also a professional nurse throughout the night.

Looking downstream from the east abutment showing from left to right Fishermans Wharf, Embarcadero, Mission Dolores, and Twin Peaks.

Wreckage with part of an impinged victim showing.

The tumbleweed which Hecox saw on the tracks. The men are Southern Pacific section hands from Carlin.

A body within the wreckage.

Later in Oakland, Thelma refused to be recognized as a heroine. Her one concession after the ordeal had been acceptance of the compartment of a passenger who was less tired than she. Even for that she felt guilty.

"As soon as I get some rest I'll be back on my run again," she smilingly told reporters. A few days later, she gave the following modest deposition to Southern Pacific officials:

"San Francisco
"August 30th, 1939

"My name is Thelma Ristvedt. I am employed as a stewardess and was so employed on the City of San Francisco which was wrecked at Harney on August 12th, 1939.

Leaving Carlin I was in the observation car where I met the conductor who had some telegrams for some of the passengers on the train. There were two telegrams for persons whom I knew were in the coach. I told the conductor I would deliver them and started forward with them. I had reached the center of the club car when I felt a rather severe lurch to the right as though we were going around a rather sharp curve. The next instant there was a terrible crash and grinding sound. Something hit me on the right side of the head and I believe I was knocked unconscious for a few moments.

Alex Fustos, one of the train employees helped me from the car which was in the creek bed. Thereafter I assisted with the injured as best I could.

The night was very dark, there being little moon out. Shortly after the crash, some of the men built fires which helped the situation out some.

I worked with the people for some time until I apparently fainted. I was then taken to a car where the injured were being treated. It was still dark at that time and I remained in that car until the relief train arrived.

I was probably on the East side of the river at some time during the night but I have no recollection of being in the vicinity of where the original point of derailment was. I can not give any information whatever about the condition at that point as I did not see it."

★   ★   ★

The most heroic moment to Dr. Brigham came when in the midst of great suffering a Black porter smiled through his own excruciating pain and asked that "the passengers be attended to first."

"I don't even know his name," Brigham told reporters the next day in San Francisco. "His was one of the worst torn bodies in the wreck. The porter's left foot was slashed away at the ankle. His

The track conditions west of the bridge. A relief train is in the background.

Special agents and other Southern Pacific personnel looking for evidence under the rear section of the Union Square, the point of the derailment. At this spot the tampered track joint was found.

Awaiting the removal of the bodies to Oakland, California.

Relatives and friends waiting for the survivors in the Oakland terminal.

The Mission Dolores.

Looking west at the wreckage in the river bed south of the bridge and the south side of the temporary trestle.

upper leg was broken so bad the thigh bone protruded from the wound. His shoulder also was crushed and broken. I have never seen such a case of self-denial. 'Don't bother with me, Doc. Tend to the passengers first,' he implored. That was heroism one doesn't meet in my profession or any other very often. I stopped the flow of blood from his ankle and I gave him first aid before he made me move on. That man's smile carried me through what was an awful night."

On vacation from Northeast Deaconess Hospital in Boston, the physician was starting a vacation trip to build up his own health. Sitting in a compartment all alone on the relief train because he was exhausted, survivors thanked Providence he was aboard the ill-fated train. Without him, the death toll would have tripled.

Brigham had to fight his own way out of a jammed compartment flooded to the level of the berth with water from the Humboldt River in order to aid the stricken passengers. He worked with only a small emergency kit, easing pain and treating the

worst-injured until his supply of medicines and sedative gave out.

Modestly he refused to take credit for what he had done. He gave more credit to a battered little brown flashlight that he carried in his coat pocket than to himself.

"This saved a lot of lives," he said, looking at the light.

Brigham described how he was imprisoned in his compartment in the first car behind the club car. Tired by 8:00 p.m. that night, he had gone to bed. The streamliner had just slipped out of Utah and was now well into Nevada. His porter, "a nice little fellow," wished him good night and promised to wake him in the morning.

The next time the doctor saw him, the porter was dead in the companionway outside the compartment. Half his head had been crushed in.

When the train plunged over the brink of the river, Brigham had been awakened by the crash. He tried his compartment door, but found it jammed. Then he thought of his flashlight. For an hour

Peering through the west end door of the Mission Dolores interior.

and a half he worked to free himself. Then with the flashlight as a club, he broke the glass of the car window and climbed out.

A bridge girder had literally ripped through the compartment next to his. Brigham used the girder as a ladder to climb up the car and break into the next above compartment. Had not the compartment been empty, he realized, the girder would have crushed those sleeping there.

Still using the flashlight as a bludgeon, Brigham broke into compartment after compartment, finally climbing into a car to treat the injured passengers inside. In this compartment he found a father in an upper berth pinning down upon his crushed son in the lower berth. Efforts to free the two wedged them only more tightly together as the heavy metal car above it ground further into the train. Father and son waited four hours before they were released.

"I treated everyone I could in my car and then climbed out to help with the survivors who had been removed. It was the most horrible sight I ever saw and remember that I was with the Medical Corps in the World War. They were horribly mutilated. I saw fractures where the broken limbs could be turned completely around."

Brigham still planned to follow through with his vacation plans of visiting the Golden Gate International Exposition and then flying to Canada for some horseback riding.

★　★　★

The only man to come out alive from the dining car unit (named by passengers as the "death car") said it all happened too fast for him to recall.

James Hanna, a steward, had only a few scratches on his hands and face. He explained that

he and 18 other men rode the speeding section into the river canyon. All other 18 died.

"I was sitting at a table writing my reports for the day. Everything was going so quietly I don't even remember what part of the car I was in. The other stewards were moving about cleaning up the other tables. Our last patron had left half an hour before. Suddenly there was a terrific jerk. I was thrown headlong. Then I was tossed back and jammed against something, I don't know what, as the lights went out. It seemed that the whole car collapsed around me."

All three units of the dining car section had been crushed like an accordion. The cooks riding in the center car of the three were killed instantly when the train was whipped broadside against a concrete abutment. Hanna said he was stunned momentarily but awakened and climbed out of the wreckage, aiding several in a climb toward the starlight they saw on one side. That was where the entire top of the train had been ripped away by the impact.

They slipped out of the wrecked diner and into the river, which at that point was only a foot deep. Later he found men and women he had helped dead and covered with sheets. Coroner's deputies said many of them had died of shock.

Hanna joined the train crewmen administering first aid and helping build fires for the survivors who had been carried out of the wrecked cars.

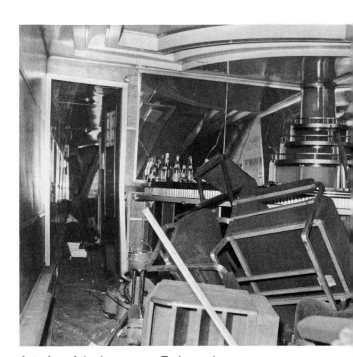

Interior of the lounge car Embarcadero.

This photograph is looking west along the inside of the curve. The side of the car in the left foreground is that of Union Square where the misalined track was found.

"I watched men, the cowboys and CCC boys and other volunteers, climb 70 and 80 feet of slippery sides of those metal cars breaking windows to let out other survivors. The ranchers came from near and far. They brought their axes to chop into the train and help those people out. I saw Alex Fustos, one of our cooks who got out, working right with them and some of the passengers didn't get out of their compartments for 3 or 4 hours."

★ ★ ★

Limping from a cut heel, Phillip Short was proud that he had rescued two women in the wreck. Returning from a visit to his parents in Boston, Short had taken the City of San Francisco because he had not been able to get reservations in Chicago on the tourist streamliner, "The Challenger."

"I like to play cards, so I sat up in the club car most of the way. Fifteen minutes before the wreck I decided to get some sleep, so I went back to the day coach and stretched out. Moving back to the day coach saved my life, I guess. I was just dozing off when there was a sound like thunder. Then our car went over on its side. A moment later fumes which must have come from some sort of refrigeration or air conditioning machine began to fill the car.* I crawled toward the front of the car. As I passed the door to the women's dressing room I heard screaming. I crawled in and found two women. One of them was trying to break the window with the heel of her slipper. I got alongside her and kicked the window, cutting my heel. Then I took her slipper and knocked off the jagged pieces of glass from the window frame. I helped one of the women through the opening, crawled through myself and pulled the other woman after me."

*Southern Pacific officials said gas used in the train's refrigeration system is odorless, non-poisonous, noninflammable. The "fumes" may have been caused by lack of air due to the destruction of the air-conditioning system.

61

Looking downstream showing demolished bridge and sabotaged streamliner. Cars Golden Gate Park and Seal Rock are to the left, with Chinatown protruding over the bridge's twisted steel.

Looking east through the bridge at the 12th crossing of the Humboldt River. This bridge, the track, and guard rail are exactly of the same construction of that of the collapsed bridge.

Looking east showing diner Mission Dolores in the foreground. Embarcadero is in the background, with Twin Peaks and Chinatown to the left. Fishermans Wharf is in the center background.

★ ★ ★

All participants agreed that the hundreds of deeds of heroism that marked the night's tragedy were overshadowed by the orderly manner in which all passengers and crewmen accepted the terrible crash.

There was none of the continuous screaming and chaos often connected with such tragedies. Each person seemed to realize that each had to do his share in meeting all the discomfort. All accepted the situation calmly and without hysteria, even after the initial shock passed.

"I did not hear a single scream," said Mrs. A. Moller of Berkeley. "I was awakened, of course, by the crash. Although I wasn't injured, I was frightened, especially when I found the train in total darkness in a mountain canyon. But everyone else was taking it quietly, so my fears were allayed. There was no panic."

Mrs. Moller, a buyer for a Berkeley department store, was en route home from New York, were she

had been selecting stocks for the new seasons. She had crossed the continent many times, but this was her first mishap.

Mrs. Helen C. Meiklejohn, whose husband, Alexander, was a professor with the University of Wisconsin, was in her berth, but not asleep when the crash came. She was thrown into the aisles, banging her nose and eyes, and then remained pinned for hours while volunteer workers tried to release her.

"I never was so glad to see anyone as I was the cowboy who finally climbed in and freed me. I had been bleeding all the while, though it wasn't serious and I never was unconscious. The cowboys helped me climb out of the train and up a girder to land."

Miss Mary Winne, a Honolulu school teacher, described the arrival and rescue by the cowboys.

"There was a terrific banging and clattering as the car went over the bank. I was in the first

63

View from the bottom of the embankment near west abutment showing tangled wreckage of the Presidio car.

Southern Pacific personnel examine the wreckage of the bridge and Presidio.

sleeper car to dive into the canyon and I felt the car fall to pieces. The crash ripped the top off as if it were paper, and then the bottom drooped away. But I had to break a window to get air. I lay there for four hours, hardly able to move. Finally some cowboys pried their way into my compartment and put a rope around me. They lowered me down the slippery side of the car to the river bed, where I was able to scramble to a fire."

The pains taken by the Southern Pacific to care for the survivors, both those who were injured and those who were not, appealed to Miss Helen Wilkinson and her sister, Eda, both traveling to San Francisco for their vacation from Evanston, Ill. The two women were in their berths when the train plunged into the river.

Helen Wilkinson was thrown to the floor and pinned there by her berth. She managed to scramble free and remained in the car, which was one of the three that did not leave the track. At daylight, they were taken into Carlin and given breakfast.

"I believe they kept us in the cars so we wouldn't see the horrible sights outside. They must certainly have been too gruesome for women's eyes. We're both terribly thankful to be alive."

★　★　★

The twisted beams of the damaged bridge. The broken and battered body of the Presidio is on the left.

The west end of Fishermans Wharf is shown next to the lower end of the Chinatown.

The Chinatown rests on the crushed end of the car Twin Peaks.

The broken east end of the Twin Peaks with the Chinatown resting upon it.

Interior of Market Street.

Wreckage.

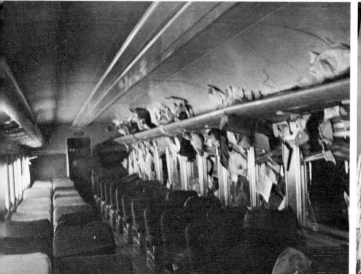

After telephoning for doctors, ambulances, and help of every kind, Hecox, followed by a corps of railroadmen and townsfolk, started back to the death scene with a grim realization of what had befallen his charges.

A scene of indescribable horror confronted him as he reached the wreck. By the dim light of lanterns and torches, he beheld a sight of havoc, though the mounting shrieks of pinioned people alone were enough to tell the story. Here and there he could see the dead and injured. And all about him little knots of men, passengers and crewmen, worked to help others less fortunate than themselves. Hecox and his companions immediately pitched in, working frantically, extricating some, muttering words of hope to others.

It was not long before ambulances arrived with doctors and nurses. Then followed wreckage crews with sheriffs and their deputies. Huge lights were thrown on the wreck. Searchlights played on the tumbled cars piled up in the stream.

Down to the water's edge men scampered with stretchers and with crowbars. Here, an arm lay extending from beneath an overturned coach.

Work is underway to remove the wreckage.

Various scenes of the wreckage.

The sad task of identifying the dead.

There, a woman frantically tried to wiggle through a window.

As the rescue work went on, it was apparent the toll in human life would be high.

Trucks and autos were pressed into service to augment ambulances. Before long, hospitals were crowded beyond capacity. Doctors' offices were turned into improvised wards.

Hours passed before the last of the injured had been removed and sent away for medical care. But long before, railroad men and peace officers dis-

covered that this had not been a railroad accident. It was a criminal act conceived and executed with fiendish care in order to wreak the maximum destruction upon the helpless streamliner with her load of passengers and crew.

By lantern light, the railed curve approaching the bridge told the harrowing story of murder. It did not take long to discover that the tracks had been tampered with — moved with devilish care to accomplish one of the cruelest crimes in American railroad history. And the imaginative rare cun-

Mrs. Floyd Romiti and her 8 month son who escaped injury. They are shown after their arrival on the relief train in Oakland, California.

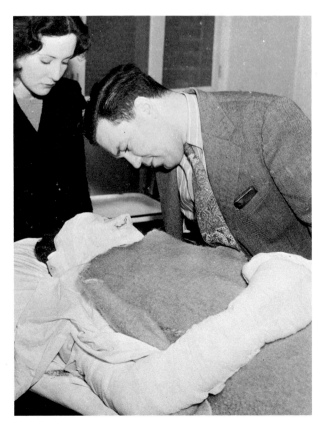

Tony Firpo in the Carlin, Nevada, hospital two days after the crash. He is being visited by Norman and Jane Anthony, close friends who travelled from Salinas, California, to see him.

ning that had gone into the derailment would not be learned until daylight allowed for a more thorough study of the rails.

★ ★ ★

There was pathos and joy, tears and smiles, in the ancient and soot-blackened Oakland passenger terminal as relatives and friends awaited the arrival of the special relief train bearing the survivors. All eyes focused on the big, black time board and its chalked notation: "Delayed train 101, the City of San Francisco, will arrive at 12:15 a.m."

But there would be none of the tan-yellow streamlined cars in the special soon to arrive. They lay in the shallow bed of the Humboldt River with a possible death toll of 40 people.

First among the women to arrive at the terminal was Mrs. Aubrey Wall of Alameda, the wife of Sam Wall, 31, a cook. Overjoyed because she knew her husband was not numbered among the fatalities, she curbed her feelings out of respect for others less fortunate.

"I could just see my husband lying in that river canyon dead when I first read the papers. Then I got word through the company that he was only injured. I thought the whole dining car was killed."

Told her husband had suffered only slight back injuries, Mrs. Wall was at the terminal to meet him. But he was not on the train. His friends re-

vealed to her that his injuries also included a broken leg and back and that he was in the hospital at Carlin.

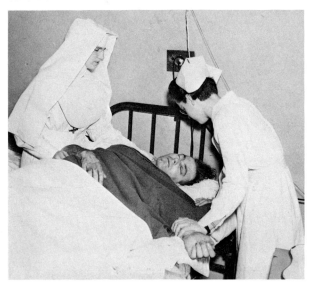

Unidentified injured passenger in the Carlin hospital.

Survivors waiting for a train to take them to Oakland. Passengers and reclaimed luggage sit on the Western Pacific track. The damaged bridge and wrecked cars are in the background.

The cruel suspense of waiting that brought no definite word cast Mrs. Harry Specht of Oakland in a tragic role.

At the time of her arrival in the passenger terminal, Southern Pacific had announced there were only 20 known dead. But only 19 had been positively identified and the 20th victim was an unidentified crew member.

And Harry Specht was a dining car cook.

Hoping against hope, Mrs. Specht waited at the terminal through the chilly morning hours until the special arrived. But her husband was not aboard. And no one on board could tell her where he was. She broke into hysterical spasms of sobbing. Friends comforted her as best they could and led her gently from the station.

Fate, however, was kind to two men who waited at the terminal to greet their friends.

One was Ed Tschumi, supervisor of menus aboard Southern Pacific's Overland, who lived in Oakland during his layovers. Four months previously, Tschumi traded places with Charles Lewis, Jr., of Alameda, and Lewis took his old job on the City of San Francisco. Lewis was one of the 20 killed.

"It was just a little thing that made me change," Tschumi recalled. "My home is Chicago, and the layover in Oakland on the streamliner job was too long. So I made the trade with Charley. And now Charley is dead."

Another man who rated himself "lucky" was Thomas Murray of Oakland, the assistant steward on the City of San Francisco dining room crew.

"I guess I just missed curtains by one trip," Murray said. "Maybe my number wasn't up. I was supposed to go out when the streamliner left here tomorrow."

Mrs. Elain Murray gripped her husband's arm tighter and said: "I'm really the lucky one."

Tschumi was also interested in knowing whether James W. Hanna, assistant steward who lived in the same apartment building with him, was aboard the special.

At that time, his fate was cloaked in uncertainty. But when the train jarred to a halt in the terminal, Hanna was among the first to clamber down.

H.W. Stewart of Palo Alto, Director of the Educational Guidance Center Summer School in Alameda, was there to meet Dr. Ernest Betts, the Penn State authority on remedial reading.

★   ★   ★

Hecox and Kelley lean on the west end of the Presidio just west of the demolished bridge.

Hecox

A derrick begins the task of lifting the demolished cars from the stream. This photograph is looking east showing from left to right Chinatown resting on Twin Peaks, wreckage of the bridge and the car Presidio on the west abutment, and the cars Golden Gate Park, Fishermans Wharf, Embarcadero, and Mission Dolores.

Rescuers resting after crawling through twisted piles of steel looking for unconscious passengers.

Chief Special Agent Dan O'Connell stands between A.D. Dyer and AH. McDonald, the president of Southern Pacific.

McDonald and a special agent observe the Embarcadero. Chinatown is in the rear background.

Scott O. Harris, foreman of the coroner's jury, is in the center studying list of the dead. Other two men are reporters.

Temporary telegraph and telephone station.

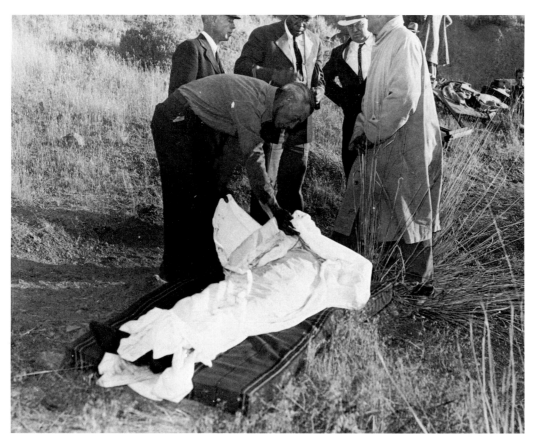

A dead passenger.

A derrick prepares to lift the Chinatown after a trestle was extended to the car.

Derrick prepares to lift Chinatown onto a flatbed car.

Derrick at work lowering the Chinatown.

Looking north from the river showing a pile driver working from the east abutment.

The derailed power units.

Lifting the Chinatown.

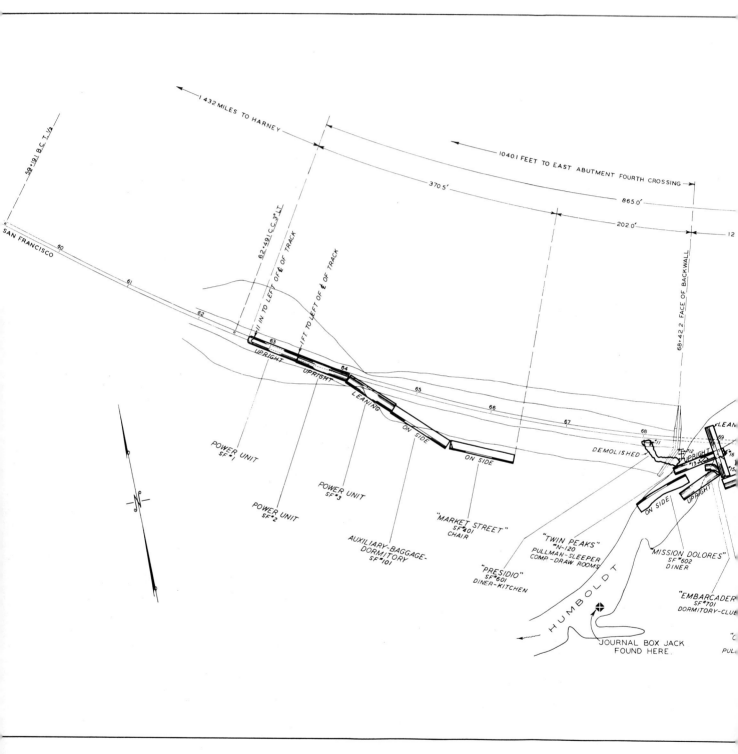

Within the drawing (labels):

1 432 MILES TO HARNEY

10401 FEET TO EAST ABUTMENT FOURTH CROSSING

370.5'

865.0'

202.0'

59+19 B.C. T.V2

62+49 I.C.C. 3° LT.

68+42.2 FACE OF BACKWALL

SAN FRANCISCO

60

61

62

63

64

65

66

67

68

69

UPRIGHT

UPRIGHT

LEANING

ON SIDE

ON SIDE

DEMOLISHED

LEAN

UPRIGHT

ON SIDE

UPRIGHT

N

POWER UNIT SF #1

POWER UNIT SF #2

POWER UNIT SF #3

AUXILIARY-BAGGAGE-DORMITORY SF #101

"MARKET STREET" SF #401 CHAIR

"PRESIDIO" SF #601 DINER-KITCHEN

"TWIN PEAKS" #N-120 PULLMAN-SLEEPER COMP-DRAW. ROOMS

"MISSION DOLORES" SF #602 DINER

"EMBARCADER SF #701 DORMITORY-CLUB

HUMBOLDT

JOURNAL BOX JACK FOUND HERE

This superb drawing was prepared by the chief engineer for Southern Pacific illustrating the embankment and excavation slopes, as well as the positions found of the tools used for the derailment.

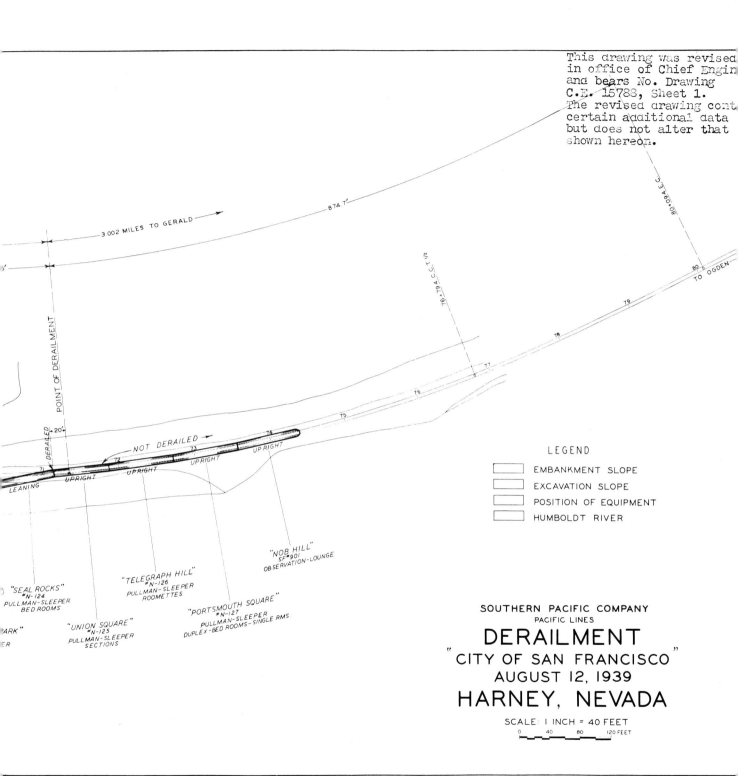

3 002 MILES TO GERALD

874 7'

80° 04' E

TO OGDEN

80

76 794 C.C.T 1/2

79

78

POINT OF DERAILMENT

77

76

75

74

73

72

NOT DERAILED

UPRIGHT

UPRIGHT

UPRIGHT

71

UPRIGHT

DERAILED

20'

LEANING

LEGEND

EMBANKMENT SLOPE

EXCAVATION SLOPE

POSITION OF EQUIPMENT

HUMBOLDT RIVER

"NOB HILL"
SF #901
OBSERVATION-LOUNGE

"TELEGRAPH HILL"
#N-126
PULLMAN-SLEEPER
ROOMETTES

"SEAL ROCKS"
#N-124
PULLMAN-SLEEPER
BED ROOMS

"PORTSMOUTH SQUARE"
#N-127
PULLMAN-SLEEPER
DUPLEX-BED ROOMS-SINGLE RMS.

"UNION SQUARE"
#N-125
PULLMAN-SLEEPER
SECTIONS

PARK"
ER

SOUTHERN PACIFIC COMPANY
PACIFIC LINES

DERAILMENT
" CITY OF SAN FRANCISCO "
AUGUST 12, 1939
HARNEY, NEVADA

SCALE: 1 INCH = 40 FEET

0   40   80   120 FEET

A pool about 400 feet downstream from the bridge where
the tools were found. Dan O'Connell points to the spot with
a willow stick. The photograph also illustrates the demolished bridge to the left and an old Southern Pacific
roadbed on the right.

Chapter 2

AUTOPSY

Chief Special Agent Dan O'Connell, who had arrived the morning after the derailment from his Southern Pacific headquarters in San Francisco, was already busy in the investigation. From Beowawe, Nevada, where he established temporary headquarters, he proceeded with several of his special agents to what remained of bridge no. 4.

After conducting an examination of the shambles, he walked up to the point where the track had been tampered. Examining the wooden ties, he observed how the tie plate on the joint ties of the receiving rail had been deliberately moved over about 4½ inches and that the spikes on the outside of the plate were down to full depth. The spikes on the inside were pulled up a distance of about 3½ inches and were now leaning slightly toward the center of the tie.

O'Connell noticed that the rail which had been the receiving rail at the joint where the track was tampered with had been moved over in a northerly direction, that is, close to the north rail of the track. Then, he spotted a mark on the outside end of that rail which evidently resulted when the flange of a wheel struck it. He also noticed that other spikes on the track had been yanked out.

Placing several of his special agents on guard over the crucial evidence, O'Connell walked over to the scene of the wreck where Hecox was talking with other crew members. The engineer explained to the agent that while approaching the point of derailment the streamliner was moving at no more than 60 miles per hour and that the power unit was riding smoothly. The automatic block signals displayed proceed indications. The headlight was focused properly and was burning brightly. As the train entered the curve beyond which was the tampered rail, he saw an object lying across the tracks about 300 feet down the line. The object was a green tumbleweed. Upon reaching that object, Hecox felt the streamliner lurch and then thud along the track. With his power unit derailed, his first thought was that the train had struck a rock. He immediately switched off power and applied the electromagnetic brakes. The train stopped within a distance of 900 feet. It was clear and dark, although the time was only 9:33 p.m. Hecox added that he felt the track was in excellent condition.

After stopping, the engineer quickly examined the pilot but found there were no marks indicating that it had struck a rock. Power unit no. 1 was

Looking east at the leaving end of the south rail of the point of derailment. The tie plate was shifted inward to hold the receiving rail in the derailing position. Man under the car is roadmaster Harry Williamson. Note that the nut and spring washer have been removed for the bolt of the joint. Bolt on the next tie remains undisturbed although the inside spikes have been pulled.

upright, although the left wheels were outside the left rail and the right wheels inside the right rail. The unit had been supported upon the rails and was prevented from overturning by the motor housings and spring planks. Hecox then ran toward Harney where he ordered relief trains. Within a few minutes, he returned to the scene of the tragedy. He examined the track for some distance to the rear of the train, but found no marks on the ties or rails east of the point of derailment. The green tumbleweed which had been pushed aside by the trucks was found lying near the fourteenth unit of the train and Hecox threw it over the embankment.

About eight feet down the embankment, he discovered a track clawbar. Looking under the fourteenth unit, he noticed that a rail-joint had been disconnected on the high or south rail at a point 160 feet east of the bridge. The angle-bars had been carefully removed and on the first tie west of this joint, a tie plate was secured inward about 5 inches from the normal position. Although the two outside spikes were fully driven, the two inside spikes had been driven only part way. There were about 20 loose spikes lying adjacent to the disconnected joint.

Two spikes driven halfway were at the south end of the second tie west of the joint and about 6 inches

Close up of Williamson showing outer edge of tie plate that was removed from the shoulder tie. Tie plate with 4 spikes, 2 projecting up in the air, is the respiked intermediate plate holding the receiving rail to form the derail. The tie plate on the next tie west has not been changed from the original position. The 2 spikes in this tie were used as a fulcrum to wedge over the receiving rail.

Jack Walker, a member of the Southern Pacific rescue crew, points to the spot where the connecting angle plate was removed and the spikes shifted so that the rails would spread.

distant from the tie plate which was in a normal position. A drift pin was lying near the joint. The disconnected rail was lying on its die with its base toward the north and its receiving end near the north companion rail. The two bond wires were straightened out, stretched in a northwesterly direction, and torn loose from the receiving end of the disconnected rail, although they were still attached to the leaving rail. The ties were in their original position in the ballast.

O'Connell then showed Hecox a close-up photograph one of his agents had taken earlier in the morning under the fourteenth unit. The photograph showed that angle-bars had been removed at a rail joint and that track bolts, nuts, and tight-lock washers were lying adjacent to this joint. Track spikes had been drawn from the undisturbed tie plate at the west end of the leaving rail and all track spikes along with the tie plate had been removed from the south end of the first ties

Note holes on both sides of the tie plate under the leaving rail indicating where the spikes have been removed. Also, note the empty spike holes in the tie plate on the second tie west from the point of the derailment showing nut and spring washer removed from the bolt of the joint.

The rail in the foregound turned over with the base toward the north, or inside rail. The front casting forming the pilot of power unit no. 1 was badly scored due to the sliding on top of the rail. This scoring resulted within the back faces of the drivers.

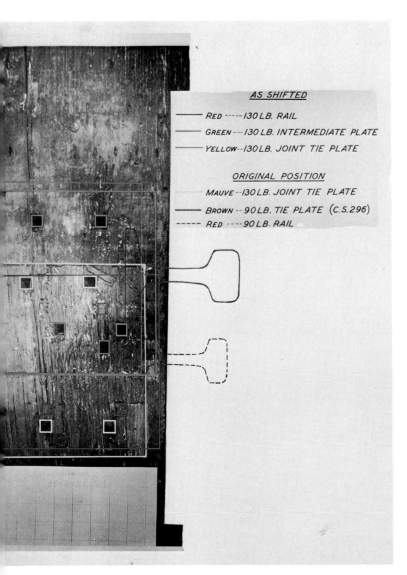

AS SHIFTED

—— RED ----- 130 LB. RAIL
—— GREEN --- 130 LB. INTERMEDIATE PLATE
—— YELLOW-- 130 LB. JOINT TIE PLATE

ORIGINAL POSITION

—— MAUVE -- 130 LB. JOINT TIE PLATE
—— BROWN -- 90 LB. TIE PLATE (C.S. 296)
---- RED ---- 90 LB. RAIL

After the rail was forced over into a derailing position and temporarily held by blocks of wood or a journal jack, the joint tie plate was inserted under the rail and a spike driven in one of the holes on the outside. The trainwreckers immediately observed that without angle bars the spikes in the joint plate would not function properly in holding down the flanges of the rail. Therefore, the spike was withdrawn and the plate removed. In withdrawing the spike, the hole in the tie was elongated. An intermediate plate removed from one of the ties westward, or secured from the roadbed, was then inserted and four spikes driven to engage the rail.

This procedure is illustrated in the following photograph. The position of the 130-lb rail used as a derailer is shown in red line. The joint plate first applied is outlined in yellow with one hole resting directly over the extra spike hole found in the tie. The intermediate tie plate that was finally applied is outlined in green and the four green holes represent the four spikes that were driven.

A close examination of the photograph shows the tops of tie plugs driven prior to the application of the 130-lb tie plate. These plugs were evidently driven at the time the 130-lb rail was laid replacing a 90-lb rail. That is, a 90-lb rail existed in the curve between 1916 and 1931. Under this rail on the 1928 cross tie was a CS 296 intermediate tie plate. The plate is outlined in brown. The two outside spike holes and one inside spike hole conform to the tie plugs that show in the photo. The position of the 90-lb rail that existed on this tie plate is outlined in broken red line. The original or normal position of the 130-lb joint tie plate that was removed is shown in purple, with holes in the plate conforming to spike holes that existed in the tie.

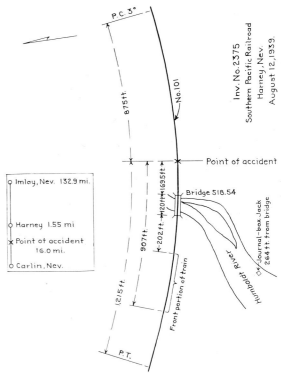

FIGURE 1.—Track lay-out in vicinity of point of accident.

The track lay-out in the vicinity of the derailment.

west of the disconnected joint. A tie-plate was placed inward about 4 or 5 inches from the normal alinement for a tie plate. There were two spikes fully driven in the two outer holes of this plate and in the two inside holes there were two spikes with their heads about 3 inches above the top of the tie. The shanks of the latter spikes were slightly bent and abraded, which indicated that they had been partially withdrawn. Several loose spikes were lying on the ballast near the south end of the ties. The ties were in alinement at their ends and were tightly secured by the ballast. The two bond wires were still attached to the west end of the leaving rail at the disconnected joint. They were straightened out and extended diagonally across the line of the track.

Hecox identified these conditions exactly as he first saw them the night before.

O'Connell next interviewed Windy, who stated that approaching the point of the derailment, he and the electrician were in the forward end of power unit no. 2. They had been attempting to start a motor when they felt skidding sensations which indicated the train was out of control. Immediately after the derailment, he and the electrician were engaged in rescue work. It was about 3 a.m. when he first had an opportunity to notice the track conditions under the fourteenth unit. Windy corroborated Hecox's statement in all essential details. At was his opinion that some force exerted pressure against the outside of the rail to move the displaced track toward the north rail. There, it had been respiked. That rail had been arranged to form a derailer.

Next, district road foreman of engines A.P. Fogus was interviewed. He, too, explained that he

Contact point on the first power unit showing damage inflicted.

85

Various views of the misalined tie-plates, bond wires, nuts, washers, and fulcrum spikes.

W.H. Kirkbride studies the journal box found in the river.

was in the second power unit at the time of derailing. Apparently, both he and Windy had left the control cab of unit no. 1 about a minute before. They were responding to a red signal indicating motor trouble in the second power unit. Before leaving the cab, Fogus noticed from the speedometer that the streamliner was cruising normally at a speed of about 60 miles per hour. At the moment of impact, he felt the wheels of the second unit strike the ties. The rough-riding action which indicated derailment frightened him very much. His unit listed considerably to the left and for a moment he felt the power unit would topple. But the car ground to a halt.

After the train stopped, Fogus immediately examined the equipment and found that the wheels of the second unit had indeed been in contact with the ties. Not only was the pilot nicked and loosened on the left front portion, but there were also marks on the first pair of wheels of unit no. 1 indicating that they, too, had been in contact with numerous objects. The motors, gear housings, and pedestal binder-bolts had been in contact with the rails and, acting as guides, prevented units 1 and 2 from leaving the track. Although the right and left wheels were about 10 inches to the left of their respective rails, the two power units were hardly damaged at all. In fact, after being replaced

A closeup of the journal box jack found in the river 260 feet downstream from the bridge.

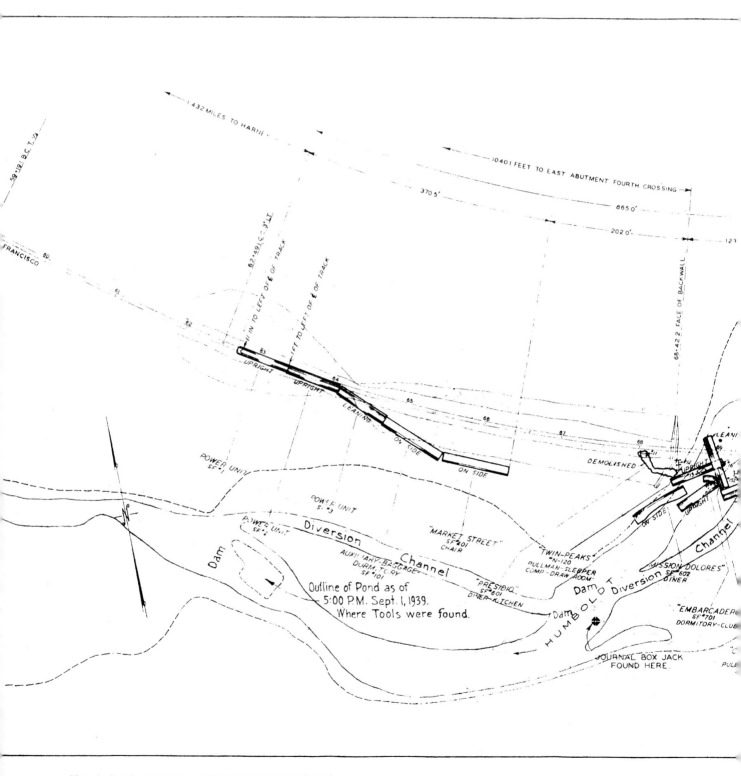

Map indicating where derailment tools were found.

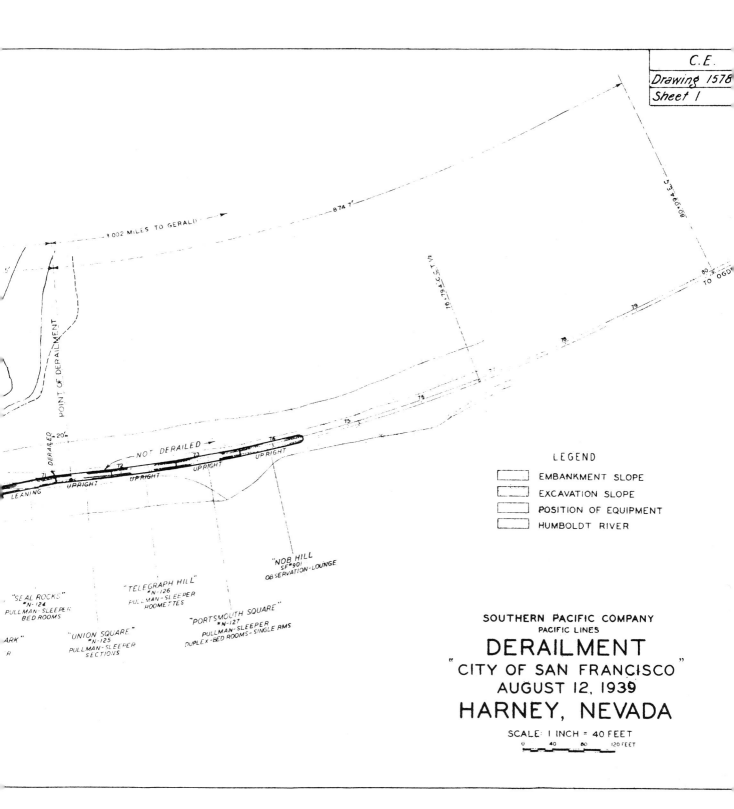

LEGEND

EMBANKMENT SLOPE
EXCAVATION SLOPE
POSITION OF EQUIPMENT
HUMBOLDT RIVER

C.E.
Drawing 1578
Sheet 1

"NOB HILL"
SF#901
OBSERVATION-LOUNGE

"TELEGRAPH HILL"
#N-126
PULLMAN-SLEEPER
ROOMETTES

"SEAL ROCKS"
#N-124
PULLMAN-SLEEPER
BED ROOMS

"PORTSMOUTH SQUARE"
#N-127
PULLMAN-SLEEPER
DUPLEX-BED ROOMS-SINGLE RMS

"UNION SQUARE"
#N-125
PULLMAN-SLEEPER
SECTIONS

SOUTHERN PACIFIC COMPANY
PACIFIC LINES
DERAILMENT
"CITY OF SAN FRANCISCO"
AUGUST 12, 1939
HARNEY, NEVADA

SCALE: 1 INCH = 40 FEET

0   40   80   120 FEET

POINT OF DERAILMENT

3.002 MILES TO GERALD

874.7'

NOT DERAILED

LEANING   UPRIGHT   UPRIGHT   UPRIGHT   UPRIGHT

TO OGD

91

The fifty foot panel of the track removed for analysis. The rail marked "leaving — outside" was the tampered joint. All of this panel is the original track existing prior to the derailment except for the left hand rail as far back as the first joint behind the man. This was the original 110 lb rail laid on the ties and plates.

on the rails a few days later, they were able to proceed under their own power. Power unit no. 3 also derailed and inclined at an angle to the left. It stopped with its front end about three or four feet above the top of the rail, with part of its rear end down the bank. Apparently, all three power units had slid along the rails.

Fogus told O'Connell that an hour after the derailment he proceeded toward the rear of the streamliner and discovered that the bridge had been totally destroyed. The last three coaches in the train remained on the rails; the fourth car from the rear, or the fourteenth unit, was upright, although her forward truck was derailed. He explained that he observed several indentations or marks on the displaced rail, probably having been

caused by some blunt object. Around the area were several loose spikes which appeared to have been freshly pulled from the ties lying near the opening made by the rail being misalined.

Electrician Joe Baumann was next to be interviewed. He explained that he was the electrician in charge of the streamliner's motors. Approaching the point of sabotage, he, too, was in the second power unit attempting to start a motor which was causing some trouble. He felt that prior to the derailment the train had been riding normally. Baumann felt the unit leave the rail, followed by a skidding sensation combined with a wobbling action. After the units came to a halt, he proceeded down into the ravine in order to aid in the rescue work. The next morning, he noticed the bond wires had been stretched diagonally across the track at an angle to the running rail. The ballast adjacent to the displaced rail was not disturbed. He found marks on the truck binder bolts and motor housings, which indicated that they had been in contact with the rails. The binder bolts and motor housings served as guides in preventing the power units from leaving the roadbed. It was his opinion that the rail in question had been moved inward and permanently secured.

Next, brakeman John Thomas told O'Connell that after leaving Carlin, a running air-brake test was made and that the brakes functioned properly en route. Approaching the point of the derailment, he was in unit no. 4. As far as he was concerned, the streamliner was riding smoothly and not in any way exceeding the speed restrictions. He had maintained a lookout around the curves and there had been no indication of defective equipment. Thomas felt a heavy brake application, followed by extremely rough riding. The unit then toppled down the embankment, stopping on its side. After the derailment, he was too busy with relief work to examine either the track or the equipment. However, his observation the next morning corroborated what Hecox had seen.

Assistant division engineer Tom Lundy was the last to be questioned by the Chief Special Agent. He stated that he arrived at the scene around 4 a.m. and that he immediately examined the track and equipment. From the initial point of derailment to a spot about 1,000 feet eastward, he found no marks or indication of dragging equipment. The derailment occurred on the south, or high rail

The receiving rail of the tampered track joint viewed from the receiving end.

View of the receiving end of the misalined rail showing flange mark on outer corner of ball.

point 170 feet east of the bridge. Lundy had prepared a hasty sketch showing the track conditions in order to illustrate his statements.

The track was laid on a 3° curve with a superelevation of 4¼ inches on the south rail. He observed that the angle bars had been removed from the joint at the point of derailment and thrown down the embankment. Near ties no. 1 and 2, he found four blocks of wood which were about 2 inches by 3 inches by 6 inches. The rail west of the joint was found lying on its side with its base toward the north and its receiving end 1⅝ inches from the north rail, pointing diagonally in a southwesterly direction across the track. The westward rail on the left side was found along the edge of the ballast and down the embankment to the south. These rails evidently had been moved by some force striking at an angle, as evidenced by marks on the receiving end of the first misplaced rail. The north rails evidently had been moved by some force striking at an angle, as evidenced by marks on the receiving end of the first misplaced rail. The north rails were undamaged and undisturbed. Starting with the third tie west of the joint, the south ends of the ties were crushed by wheels, the damage increasing progressively westward. At the time of his observations, the fourteenth unit was standing with its west end 20 feet west of the joint involved.

Side view of the rivet-set found in the stream.

The test scale arrangement on the experimental track constructed in Oakland.

The main tools used by the saboteurs. All were recovered from the Humboldt River.

How the claw fit snugly under the westerly spike.

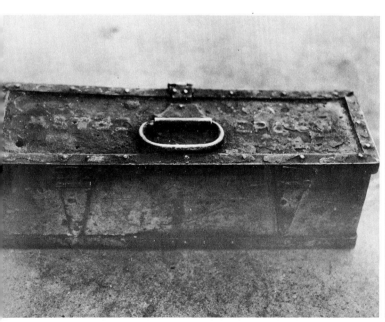

The tool box belonging to a road gang from which the tools were stolen to derail the streamliner.

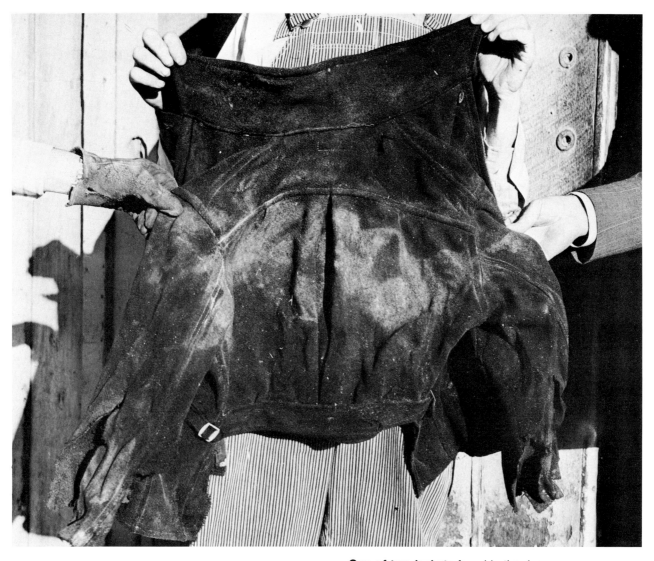

One of two jackets found in the river.

As a result of Lundy's preliminary examination, measurements were taken of the bond wires at the point of derailment. The two bond wires were straightened out and reduced in section. Not only did their condition indicate tensile strain, but the fiber suggested drawn conditions similar to those produced when metal is tested in tension. All these conditions described how the bond wires were forcibly torn away from the receiving rail. Detailed examination of the misalined tie plate disclosed that the two outer spikes were fully driven and the two inside spikes projected above the top of the tie plate. The heads of the eastward and westward spikes were 3¼ inches and 3½ inches above the tie plate.

It was possible to remove the westward spike by means of thumb and forefinger; the eastward spike was not touched. It was Lundy's conclusion that the condition of these spikes was caused by the left front wheel of power unit no. 1 as it left the leaving rail, engaging the outside surface of the ball of the receiving or misalined rail. Then, the streamliner's engine dropped to the base and ran along a distance of 20 feet before leaving the rail. This was suggested by the wheel marks starting outward in a gradual taper to a point where the marks left the rail. The pressure downward on the outer edge of the rail's ball tended to press the rail inward against the two inside spikes. This force was resisted by the rail strength being arched against the direction of the force. There was a tendency for the train to follow tangential direction with a cen-

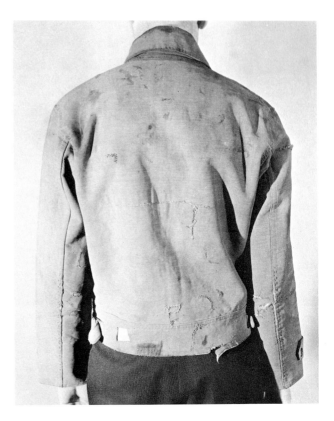

Front end of the brown jacket recovered from the river. Note unusual stitching on various parts of the coat.

Rear view of the jacket.

trifugal force in proportion to its speed of 60 miles per hour. The misalined rail, having been engaged by the pilot casting sliding upon it, was curving in a direction divergent to that of the train. Therefore, the rail could only overturn in the outward direction. Thus, observed Lundy, the result was that the eastward end of the misalined rail revolved on the tie plate under the heads of the two outside spikes. The rail flange then pulled the two inside spikes upward while yanking the two inside spikes upward sufficiently to turn clear of them.

Simultaneously, the rail was moved westward because of the friction created by the pilot casting running in contact with the ball of the rail. A movement of 10½ inches was sufficient for the rail end to clear up the spikes. Subsequent wheel blows kicked the rail inward to its final position near the north rail. The westward end of the misalined rail which was still attached to the succeeding rail was pounded into the ballast and covered by debris and equipment. The track was gaged at joints and centers a distance of 11 rail lengths eastward from the point of derailment. The south rail had a superelevation varying between 4 and 4⅛ inches, with point of derailment being 4⅛. The gage varied between 4 feet and 8½ inches at the derailing point.

In order to verify Lundy's speculations, O'Connell ordered that a series of tests be conducted in order to determine the actual strength necessary to move the rail inward. A replica of the track at the point of derailment was to be constructed in Carlin, with the only missing element being the use of sand ballast. Lundy was ordered to supervise the tests. A spring balance would be attached to measure the energy necessary to push a rail the distance the misalined rail was moved at the derailment point. Since the test could easily be administered, it would take place the very next morning.

★ ★ ★

View of the back of the flange of left no. 1 wheel of the first power showing the mark caused by striking the end of the rail.

Reilly's Free Press
August 22, 1939.

REVIEWING THE NEWS

By CIO Air Reporter

There's one thing on which we all agree. I think even the employers will agree with us on this: The world is not a very quiet or restful place to live in. Anyone who was born onto this planet believing he would have either a peaceful or orderly existence was badly mistaken. If you don't have any troubles of your own, somebody else's have a way of climbing in your window and upsetting your equilibrium.

It's like the man said when he was interviewed on the stretching rack in a torture chamber: "This is not a very comfortable place, but there's never a dull moment."

It isn't that there is any shortage of anything in this world, and it isn't that we're overcrowded. It's just that the industrialists are having a hard time making the thing pay. The world manages to go around all right, but the almighty dollar doesn't.

It isn't that the bankers and industrialists can't make money. It's just that they're too good at it. They make so dog gone much money the rest of us have the deuce of a time hanging onto a nickel. Sometimes a paycheck is like a little white bird that flies right by us. Here it comes and there it goes. We barely get time to hear it chirp.

Meanwhile, the monkeys in the cage out at the Fleishhacker zoo get along with each other far better than human beings.

Let's just take a quick look around at things.

Over in Europe, Germany is crouching on the Polish border. Hitler says hand over Danzig by September 2nd, or else. The Poles tell him to go soak his head. Britains' Chamberlain says, we won't stand for Hitler's seizing Danzig. Let's review the past warnings of the Chamberlain faction: We won't stand for Italy taking Ethiopia. We won't stand for Germany taking Austria. We won't stand for Fascist interference in Spain. We won't stand for Hitler seizing Czechoslovakia. We won't stand for Japan's insolence in China. We won't stand for Italy's seizure of Albania. It's obvious by now that Mr. Chamberlain doesn't stand for anything.

"Will there be war?" was once the leading question of the day. Now the people of the world look at the whole sorry mess of corruption and back door deals---say to themselves, "when will the bombs start dropping---when will the dogs cut loose?"

In America a giant streamlined train leaps the rails---24 dead and 119 injured.

"Sabotage," yells the Southern Pacific. "An earless maniac loosened the track. See, here is the crowbar he used."

"We see no evidence of sabotage," says the Federal Bureau of Investigation.

Along comes a workman from the S. P.'s own repair crew, takes the crowbar out of their hands. "Here, gimme that. I dropped it."

The S. P. is shaken but unabashed. "$5,000 reward for the earless maniac," they shout in every newspaper in the land.

Who is this earless maniac, deaf to the cries of human suffering? It couldn't be the - - - well, skip it. Anyhow, somebody's responsible.

A week after the derailment, Reilly's Free Press carried a bitter editorial attack on the Southern Pacific Company.

Reilly's Free Press
August 22, 1939.

RAILROADING

Until the recent terrible train wreck in Nevada, few people knew that one of the main items of railroading is running newspapers. But the blazing headlines, sensational fake stories of sabotage, twisting of rails, spiking down rails 4 inches out of line with other rails, maniac sadist wreckers and page after page of what any railroader or even anyone of common sense can see is absolutely false, proves that the "news" was manufactured to fit the railroad's orders.

In reading the first accounts, the readers question was, "are all reporters such dumbbells or are they writing under orders?" The question was settled by turning to the editorial columns of the Chronicle where the gigantic brain of Chesty Rowell heaved his mighty rolling sentences all over the page, profoundly and seriously discussing the criminality of sabotage with the possible connection of disciples of Stalin of Russia or Hitler of Germany with the case. On account of the Harry Bridges trial, Chesty did not prove that either Tom Mooney or Harry Bridges was guilty.

We are not sufficiently posted on liability laws or the funny way court decisions are made to say if running a 100 mile train on a 40 mile track would make a damage suit liability for the loss of a $2,-000,000 train belonging to another road or for the loss of the lives of 25 innocent persons. But the S.P., as usual, thought there was something to cover up and evidence must be manufactured accordingly. The S.P. detectives under the direction of O'Connell are maintained mostly for strike-breaking purposes. But they readily find the evidence required to prove the world round or flat just as needed by the railroad. If desired by the S. P., the Examiner, Chronicle or Tribune would print the proof for a round, flat, or insideout earth with plenty of photos to prove it.

O'Connell's G-men are indulging in all kinds of fool stunts worthy of the great Volmer himself. Nevada roads, what there are of them, were closed north, south, east and west. Suspects were captured, samples of dust from their clothes were compared to that of Nevada. (There must be a microscope somewhere in Nevada.) The most serious evidence found was a bunch of paper matches from some other place, found in the pocket of a cripple who had lost a foot and the use of one arm in a railroad wreck in Montana. The matches and the fact that he had never been paid any damages by the Montana railroad, was to an S.P. detective, certain proof that this cripple would wreck a train. It was only necessary to prove that he could wreck it and did wreck it.

Many people doubt if Tom Mooney was framed. The acts of the S.P. are enough to remove this doubt.

The best picture for evidence is the Examiner aerial view of Monday, August 14. This shows the engine stopped at 960 feet from the railbreak. The standard stop test is 1120 feet at 60 miles per hour. This shows that a large part of the train remained on the track for some distance having crossed the 175 foot bridge. The rear of the train was off the track and tore up the bridge.

The Examiner has it that "the murderous work of the saboteur showed plain and clear to experienced eyes." Details of just how he worked is given. (Was you dere, Sharley?) Spikes were removed and the rail-twisted sidewise four inches. In track laying this would take six men and implements. The engine is smugly on the track 960 feet away---some saboteur. The first truck of the next car is also on the track. This photo also shows two other places where the track is moved. At one place, the outer rail of the curve is pushed clear off the end of the ties for a car length. Possibly the cripple did this before making the 4-inch offset---only the S. P. detectives would know. The FBI investigators have thrown up the job, saying that there is no evidence of criminal sabotage. Only the S.P. continues on the hopes of getting a Tom Mooney goat.

This is the most dastardly piece of false newspaper frame-up work in years. Suppose an inflamed mob had hanged the innocent cripple. Who would have been guilty of murder, the mob or so-called newspapers? This only shows how many persons are tried and convicted by the newspapers before the case ever reaches a court.

The following editorials appeared in various newspapers.

The Sacramento Bee
August 15, 1939.

Justice Demands Train Wrecker Be Rounded Up

Indisputable evidence exists that the wreck of the Southern Pacific's crack streamliner, City of San Francisco, east of Reno, Saturday night, was an act of sabotage.

A fiend, nursing a murderous grudge or possessed of a warped mind from which the last vestige of mercy and honor had vanished, is believed to have planned the disaster that sent twenty three hurtling to their death in the desert night and caused the injury of 114 others.

A train wreck usually is spectacularly tragic, partly because of the nature of the equipment involved and partly because such accidents happen so seldom in these days of super safety devices, automatic signals and elaborate communication systems.

The City of San Francisco was the ultimate in modern engineering, designed to incorporate the triple factors of speed, safety and comfort. Every device known to the designers that would add to the comfort and safety of the passengers was included and extra elaborate precautions were taken to guard against accidents.

The motive for a crime so horrifying is known only to the party responsible.

But whatever it was, the murderer should be rounded up quickly and be made to pay the extreme penalty for his foul deed.

The peace and safety of organized society is menaced until this is accomplished.

Society Must Be Avenged!

Where Maniac Dealt Death, Destruction

STRONG EVIDENCE BACKS FINDING IN WRECK SAYS DOTTA

ELKO, Nev., Aug. 23 (Special)—The Southern Pacific Company built up a strong case to back its finding that the wreckage of the streamliner City of San Francisco was caused by sabotage, Mayor David Dotta of Elko said today.

Dotta, one of two business men on the company's inquiry board of five members said that the decision was supported with many facts.

"I feel that it was the only decision which could have been made in the face of the evidence presented to us," Dotta said. "It was the easiest decision I have ever been called upon to make, because of the undisputed facts to substantiate it."

Many witnesses appeared before the committee, from laymen who knew little of trains to technicians extremely well versed on the most minute details, and it was reported that none of the testimony was in conflict. The testimony established, it was said, that a niche was found in the rail which the company found was moved in, corresponding to a niche in the flange of the left front wheel of the lead power unit of the seventeen car streamliner. It was also established that spikes which had been removed from the rail were lifted out with a claw hammer, since claw hammer marks were found on them and they were straight.

What Manner of Man Would Produce a Train Wreck?

Findings of a railroad board of inquiry investigating the wreck of the Southern Pacific train invite speculation as to the identity, as well as to the mentality of the person or persons responsible for the calamitous disaster. That it was the deliberate act of a person with criminal intent is undoubted by the railroad board. What type of person is most likely to perpetrate so heinous a crime?

One thinks at first of the various mental disorders which might so distort a person's judgment as to eclipse or cancel his full realization of the consequences of such an act. The normal mind, given the momentary free play of its imagination, might conceive such a plot; but only the defective or distorted mentality could execute it. It is very unlikely that the crime was planned by a dull or a feeble-minded person; the timing, the location, and the diabolical subtlety of the mechanical arrangements suggest a normal, if not a more-than-average intelligence.

Another possibility is that it was the work of an insane person. As insanity is generally defined, that is, a demented or a maniacal person, this theory has little to support it. If by insanity is meant, however, that rare but most dangerous form of mental disease, paranoia, then we have a quite plausible explanation. In this condition, the sufferer shows no signs of disturbance or dementia, but reveals in his behavior, a consuming conviction of persecution, with a concomitant scheme to "get even" with his or her actual or imagined persecutors. The irony of this type of mental disease is that, while it is the most dangerous form of insanity known, it is the least recognizable.

Another possibility is that the act was that of a neurotic person suffering from what the authorities call a compulsion neurosis; a mental disorder less marked than either mental deficiency or mental disease. People of this type are prone to commit acts which, in their rational moments, they would never undertake. The kleptomaniac, the pyromaniac and the dypsomaniac are said to belong to this category.

This most recent of our major transportation tragedies is a dramatic reminder that our power age has not yet invented adequate moral brakes. It is a reminder, too, that the protection of life and property is, after all, dependent upon morality; and that society is no safer than the conscience and sense of social responsibility of the so-called average person.

How shall we make our new world morally fool-proof?

UNION FAVORS WRECK PROBE

Faulty Equipment Is Hinted in N. Y.

NEW YORK, Aug. 23.— (U.P.)— The Hotel Restaurant Employes Union (AFL) asked Attorney General Frank Murphy Wednesday to investigate the wreck in Nevada of the streamliner, City of San Francisco, on grounds it may have been caused by faulty equipment and neglect of the road.

George E. Brown, international vice-president of the union, said in a letter to Murphy that railroad workers can give "conclusive proof" that economies by the railroad industry have resulted in improper servicing of equipment.

"Passenger and freight equipment," Brown said, "are kept in service day after day without proper inspection or repair.

"We believe this to be an important, if not a major factor, in the wreck of the ill-fated streamliner," he added.

Brown demanded the investigation on the basis of "other disgraceful conditions prevailing throughout the industry," and said that economy reductions had resulted in personnel reductions "far below that necessary to maintain a high standard of safety."

The union, claiming 12,000 dining car workers on 50 class I railroads including the Southern Pacific and Union Pacific, part owners of the wrecked train, discounted the theory that sabotage caused the accident in Nevada that killed more than 20 and injured nearly 100.

The Deseret News
August 24, 1939.

$5000 REWARD

SOUTHERN PACIFIC COMPANY

Will Pay a Reward of FIVE THOUSAND DOLLARS ($5,000) for information leading to the arrest and conviction of person or persons responsible for wrecking train No. 101 "Streamliner City of San Francisco" near Harney, Nevada, about 9:30 p. m. Saturday, August 12, 1939.

Information should be furnished to D. O'CONNELL, Chief Special Agent, Southern Pacific Company, 65 Market Street, San Francisco, California, or to THE OFFICES OF THE FEDERAL BUREAU OF INVESTIGATION, U. S. Department of Justice, 111 Sutter Building, San Francisco, California, or 301 Continental Bank Building, Salt Lake City, Utah.

J. H. DYER
Vice-President in Charge of
Operations

SOUTHERN PACIFIC COMPANY
San Francisco, California.

August 15, 1939.

Aug. 15, 1939

HEROES AND A MANIAC

The shock of the tragedy that happened to the City of San Francisco streamliner may be somewhat relieved by dramatic stories of heroism. It is incredible that anyone but a psychopathic individual could have ripped loose a rail, reset it four inches inward, thus plunging the cars into the Humbolt River and causing an appalling human toll.

High on the list of heroes should be the name, although it remains unknown, of the Negro porter who asked the doctor to attend to the passengers first, despite the fact that he was in excruciating pain from a broken leg. Then also should be mentioned the Pennsylvania professor who saved the lives of at least 30 persons by binding the wounds of the victims. Had it not been for the Boston physician who exhausted himself caring for the maimed, there would have been greater loss of life. A great feat was performed by the Oakland porter who waded time and time again to the river to carry half-conscious persons to safety.

To the passengers should go credit for the calmness which they showed, and to the train crew praise who showed efficiency and courage all during the catastrophe.

Such stories as these will fortify one's faith in sympathy, kindness and courage of most human beings.

Broken ends of bond wires.

The cap of the paint can from which came the paint used to cover the misalined rail end.

On the following day, the tests revealed that the energy expended was as follows:

Number of ties with inside spikes pulled	Movement of rail inward	
	4 inches	4½ inches
	Pounds	Pounds
8	709.5	742.5
10	445.5	495
11	363	412.5
12	313.5	363

Using a simple 10 inch journal jack, the test was accomplished with such ease that the jack ratchet was operated without a bar. A 10 inch journal jack could readily be inserted between the spikes which were 8¼ inches from the end of tie no. 2 and the ball of the rail. The entire test was conducted in less than six minutes. It included uncoupling the joint angle bars, pulling the inside spikes from eight ties, and moving the rail inward 4½ inches. Lundy used a track-lining bar to move the rail.

Roadmaster Andy Williamson who was present during the tests told O'Connell that his last inspection of the Nevada track was on the morning of August 11 when he rode over it on a motor car. Ten days prior to this, a walking inspection had been made. In both instances, the track at the derailment curve was in excellent condition.

Williamson, who had arrived at the scene of the tragedy around 11:30 p.m., verified Lundy's statements in all essential details. The bond wires extended diagonally across the track and the ballast was undisturbed. There had been no authorized movement of ties at this spot for more than 18 months. Loose spikes, slightly bent and lying adjacent to the normal location of the south rail, displayed claw-bar marks. And, most crucial of all, as far as Williamson was concerned, the top of the ball of the misplaced rail had recently been painted with dark brown paint. Dry when examined closely the next morning, it suggested to the roadmaster that the trainwrecker wanted to prevent the streamliner's light beam from reflecting off the rail end, thereby giving it away.

★ ★ ★

Section foreman Aldo Bianchini who arrived at the scene an hour after the derailment was questioned that afternoon by O'Connell. He explained that he had been over the track just the day before and that it was in excellent condition. However, there were some tools missing from an iron box assigned to his road gang. Also, the last train which crossed over the point of derailment prior to the arrival of the City of San Francisco was a west-bound freight shortly after 6:00 p.m., or about 3 hours and 30 minutes before the sabotage.

Tool markings on one of the spikes.

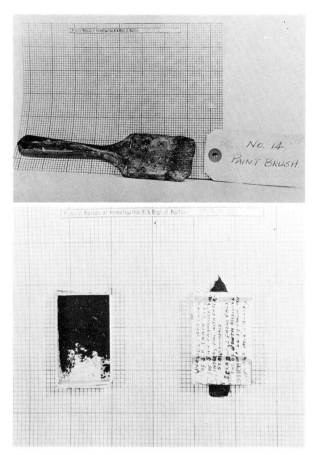

Photograph of end of the bond wire.

Sample of the paint scraped from the displaced rail.

Four track bolts with their bolt nuts and spring washers.

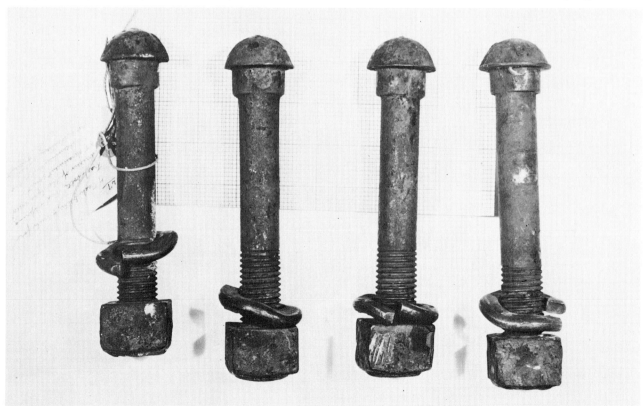

The left leading edge of the pilot car from which paint samples were taken. They matched with the paint on the rail joint.

O'Connell was then shown that a rail detector-car had gone over the track on June 19, 1939. The previous inspection was back in October of 1938, an interval of 8 months.

Bridge foreman James Stone informed O'Connell that on August 5, a week before the tragedy, he had completed the work of reinforcing the bridge and that it was in excellent condition.

That evening, O'Connell met with the president and vice president of Southern Pacific, A.H. McDonald and A.D. Dyer, in order to go over all the facts. Both had just arrived by special train from San Francisco. With the sun descending in the background, the three men met in an improvised tent a few yards from the point of derailment. A transcript of that meeting shows the following conversation:

"First, and most important of all, we know we have a mass murderer on our hands. There is not one tangible clue as to who the killer is. Rounding up suspicious characters will not solve this crime," said McDonald in calling the

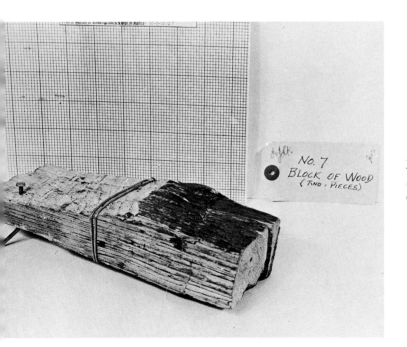

A block of wood used by the trainwrecker was found on the south side of the track near the point of the derailment. It consists of two pieces of wood tied together with a nail driven through.

The footprint found 108 yards west of the bridge.

meeting to order. "We've got to uncover some physical evidence, a few real clues. We must find . . ."

O'Connell interrupted, "We're turning the whole countryside upside down."

"Yes, and we're just beginning," Dyer added. "Heavy tools were used to move those rails and the man or men who did it certainly didn't take their tools with them. They had to be hidden somewhere. We haven't discovered them because we haven't had time to look. Chances are, they also hid the clothing they worked in. Those are the kinds of clues we must have. And, they probably are not too far distant from this very spot."

O'Connell speculated, "The river stream is the most logical place where the tools and equipment would be hidden. We'll start first thing in the morning rounding up the most professional swimmers and divers Nevada has to offer. We may even have to dam up the stream in order to dig into the river bottom. I

don't think we'll find clues beneath the wreckage. My hunch is that if there are clues, they are in the stream. These saboteurs knew what they were doing. They were professional train men. They wouldn't be stupid to leave clues scattered about. No. The stream will reveal what we are looking for."

Walking over to the entrance of the tent and watching the sun descend below the western mountain ranges, McDonald said, "Comb the entire river bed. Search the desert for a campsite. We'll take any clues we can get. Dan, I know your men have been beating the brush and side stepping rattlesnakes all day. But we've only begun. I suppose the most crucial piece of evidence would be a footprint. In the D'Autrement job, the robbers not only left a campsite, but also a pair of overalls. And you know what happened then . . ."*

O'Connell, McDonald, and Dyer, along with their assistants, spent the rest of the night pouring over the known facts. The fact that hurt the most

109

was that the total loss of life now numbered 24: nine passengers, two train-service employees, 11 dining-car workers, and two porters.

*McDonald was recalling the famous case in 1923 when three young brothers dynamited a passenger train in Oregon's Siskiyou Mountains. Several employees were killed. Several months later, a few fir needles, some grains of sand, and fingernail trimmings were discovered in the pencil pocket of an abandoned pair of overalls. Famed University of California criminologist O.H. Heinrich broke the case and yielded the identity of the murderers.

★ ★ ★

Early the next morning as the three top Southern Pacific officials scanned the stream, six stalwart, husky men came trooping up carrying swimming trunks. Tom Carpenter, the agent assigned the previous evening to rounding up the best divers and swimmers in the area, said, "Right here we have the best men Nevada has to offer. They are not afraid of water or long hours."

Heel print from the FBI heel print files. These heels correspond to those found near the bridge.

A plaster cast of the shoeprint found 2¼ miles northwest of the derailment site.

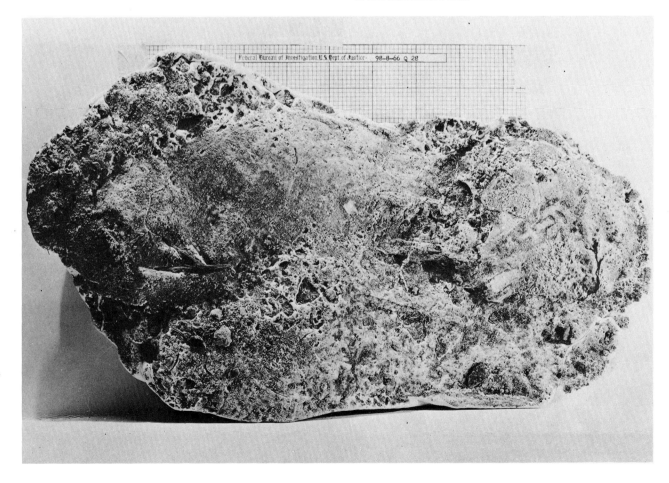

The special divers Southern Pacific recruited to search the river bottom. From left to right, Grant Stevenson, Dennis Willmore, Jesse Walker, and Fred Gasaway exhibit the track wrench Stevenson found.

O'Connell smiled. "Boys," he said after a pause, "start diving. There's the spot. You are to dive, search, and drag the river for 1000 yards in both directions. Any metal object such as a tool is to be brought up immediately. We don't care how slow the work takes. We might be here for months. But we have to find the murder weapons."

The men began their diving shortly before 8:30 a.m. But it was not until nearly quitting time that their first efforts bore fruit. Around 5:00 p.m. that afternoon, a waving arm came out of the middle of the stream. It was followed by a call for help.

"There is some kind of a large tool down here! It's snagged in the mud. I need help to bring the thing up."

A few seconds later, O'Connell and several of his agents were on the spot. Three divers were just dragging in a jack capable of moving 25 tons. O'Connell studied it closely. Finally, he looked up and smiled, "This is an excellent beginning. It looks like it might have come from the missing tools of the railroad gang. That chest was rifled on the east end of the bridge a few days before the wreck. Rush this thing to the FBI laboratories in Washington. I'm positive it has a story to tell."

"What do you want us to do now?" asked a swimmer.

"Just keep on diving. You still have a half hour before dark. Plan on being back here tomorrow morning. We need every inch of that river bottom checked and double checked. You'll be paid well. But you must keep diving, day after day, month after month. It's going to be tedious work. But the clues are in that stream."

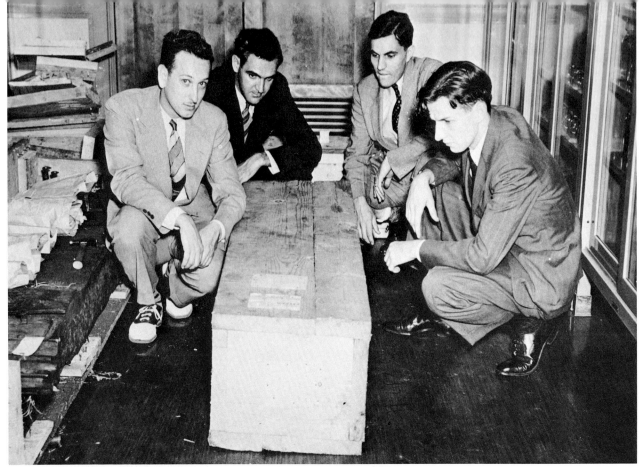

Railroad detectives examine the shipping case in which clues were received at the Southern Pacific headquarters in San Francisco.

The spot where Dan O'Connell theorized the saboteurs watched the derailment. Suspect footprints were found nearby.

The suspected avenue of getaway by the trainwreckers.

An elevated view of the wrecked cars loaded on flat cars. From left to right are the Embarcadero, Chinatown, Twin Peaks, all damaged beyond repair. Some have been cut in sections for shipping convenience.

Chapter 3

MANHUNT

The next morning, O'Connell lost no time in launching the manhunt. While the river steadily refused to yield any other clues that day, the Chief Special Agent and his men busied themselves in a myriad of details. A roundup of suspects had begun the previous day. Now, it was gaining momentum as it went along. Railroad detectives, sheriffs, and their deputies were using every available telephone and telegraph to issue orders in the dragnet.

To big cities across western America flashed instructions to learn the whereabouts of known train wreckers released from prison. Not a stone was being left unturned.

"Search railroad yards, hobo jungles, rooming houses," O'Connell ordered. "Bring in every man who can't give a satisfactory account of himself."

Throughout Arizona, Nevada, and Eastern California, highways and dirt roads were blocked by squads of deputies and volunteers. Everyone was stopped and questioned. Railroad depots and bus terminals were patrolled for suspicious characters. By noon, the hunt spread fanlike over northern California, Oregon, and Idaho. Police in big cities joined with small town constables in a thorough, determined manhunt. Time and again hopeful news flashed over the wires to O'Connell. The first major arrest was of a 28 year old "man without ears" who was said to be bitter against all railroads. Supposedly, he had been mutilated and cheated out of money. Arrested for questioning in Sparks, Nevada, all were hopeful this might indeed be the saboteur.

Andy Willever, Reno's Chief of Police, said the man's name was Bob LaDucuer. A book of paper matches had been found in his pocket from a restaurant in Frenley, Nevada. Frenley is located east of Reno and on the railroad line toward Carlin.

Short, thin, and with sparse blond hair, the man had no left foot and wore no right shoe. His ears were so small and deformed they appeared to have been cut off.

Police throughout Nevada had been ordered by radio and teletype to search and hold such a man. It seems that a "man without ears" had been seen early on the morning after the derailment peering from a ridge down into Palisade Canyon filled with the wreckage and its dead and injured. William Judice, a Carlin deputy sheriff, ordered him to come down, but the man darted back into the rugged terrain and disappeared. The same man was seen later that afternoon in Hazen, Nevada, a railroad stop some 40 west of the wreck. Covered with the alkali dust of the area, he seemed nervous and tense. An hour later, he turned up in Frenley where he appeared frightened. Hesitantly he asked motorist questions about the tragedy. Those who spoke to him were struck by his most distinguishing feature, a lack of ears. They appeared to be nothing more than disfigured rudiments stuck grotesquely on the sides of his head. LaDucuer was said to be driving a dilapidated car. He appeared to be a young man, weighing approximately 135 pounds.

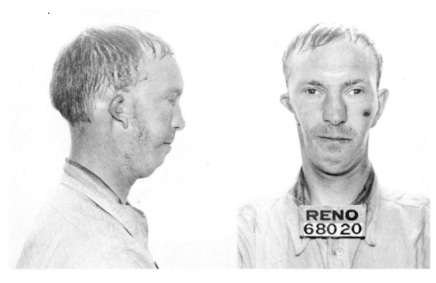

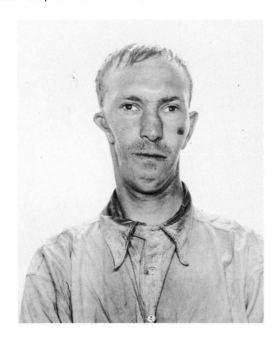

Bob LaDucuer, the so-called "earless man," was the chief suspect until the FBI cleared him.

After his arrest, dust from his clothing was rushed to a University of Nevada laboratory in Reno for comparison with the dust and sand from the Humboldt River country. Soon came a chemist's report clearing LaDucuer and he was released.

Meanwhile, two Michigan tourists told police they overheard an intoxicated railroad employee in a Wells, Nevada, cafe say on the day after the derailment:

"Southern Pacific never gave me a break. I've worked as a railroad man since the war, but I never got anything."

Then in a fit of rage, the man touched a match to his railroad cap and hurled the flaming missile through the crowded room.

The man was dressed in blue denim, had dark hair, and weighed about 160 pounds. Police speculated he was the same person W.K. Fraed of Alto Luma, California, saw near Hazen who spoke openly of his bitter feud with Southern Pacific. That unidentified former employee disappeared the night after the derailment and was never brought in for questioning.

The search continued, hour after hour. A hobo in Southern California looked "hot" for that night, but he too was quickly able to prove his innocence. In the Northwest, railroad agents began hunting for a former inmate of an insane asylum. Once before he had participated in an attempted train derailment.

And so it went. It was an endless scurrying for suspects, with disappointment at every turn. In half a dozen states, hundreds of men were being picked up because they looked suspicious, or acted in a way to arouse curiosity. Hour by hour, day by day O'Connell's work was steady and determined, an immediate, far flung hunt for anyone who might be remotely involved.

Men and women living in the sparsely settled region of the sabotage, or in the nearby little towns, were quickly interviewed in the hope they might have seen or heard something suspicious.

"If only someone had seen a loiterer around the bridge," O'Connell remarked, "We'd have someone in particular to look for. This groping in the dark is awful. But we'll get a clue sometime. Maybe it'll come out of the river. I think the saboteur either was frightened away by the horror of the wreck, or by the fact that enough men survived uninjured to make looting impractical if indeed that was his motive."

★　★　★

Railroad detectives from the Santa Fe who aided in the investigations.

Police units which aided in the search of suspects.

Two days after the derailment, J. Edgar Hoover, Director of the Federal Bureau of Investigation in Washington, D.C., issued instructions to San Francisco's FBI office to undertake the investigation. Special Agents L.H. Richmond and M.J. Cassidy were ordered to proceed immediately to the wreck scene. Arriving at 6:30 p.m. on August 14th, they conferred with McDonald, O'Connell, Dyer, and other special agents, as well as with William Jeffers, President of the Union of Pacific Railroad, who had arrived on the same day.

Also, Jay C. Newman from the FBI office in Salt Lake City headed toward the wreck area. On the following day, J.T. McLaughlin, G.V. Diernst, Lish Whitson, C.H. Olson, and C.E. Weeks reported to

Elko, Nevada, from Washington, D.C., where a temporary FBI office was established in an abandoned store.

By this time, a considerable part of the wreckage had been cleared away from the scene in order to permit track and bridge replacements. The first two ties west of the point of derailment, along with tie plates and other clues, were moved to Carlin where they were placed in O'Connell's custody.

In addition to the train passengers, employees, and rescue workers, it was estimated that over 3,000 people had visited the wreck scene on Sunday, August 13th. Many of them stole or promiscuously handled articles lying around the scene. As in other catastrophes, articles strewn around were

picked up as souvenirs. This worried O'Connell since a valuable clue might wind up on someone's shelf as a curio.

It was not until late Sunday afternoon that sufficient railroad detectives, deputy detectives, and other police officers arrived to control the crowds.

★   ★   ★

It had been the experience of Southern Pacific police as well as that of the police departments on other railroads that the usual motives for committing a malicious derailment were as follows:

1. To gain revenge for a grievance, real or imagined, against the particular railroad, or some individual connected with that railroad;
2. To loot the mail, express, or passengers after the train had been wrecked;
3. Or, to simply act out a criminally insane impulse.

With the first clues and items of information coming in, each of these three motives was given careful consideration.

In the fourth day of the investigation, O'Connell was approached by Southern Pacific personnel. In the strictest confidence, several engineers felt that it was possible the train had been wrecked in an abortive attempt to kill Hecox. O'Connell and the FBI immediately interviewed the engineer. When Hecox was asked about the possibility that someone wanted to kill him, he laughed out loud. Then, turning serious, he assured O'Connell and the FBI that this couldn't be the case since he didn't know of anyone who might want him dead. No one had ever threatened him.

Hecox was asked whether he had any family difficulties. Casually, he mentioned that the only unpleasantness he ever experienced in his family was caused by Alvin McAvoy, his son-in-law. Formerly employed by the Internal Revenue in Sparks, McAvoy was involved in a narcotic case two years previously in which a former narcotic agent was indicted and convicted. As a result of that arrest, Hecox advised his daughter who had left McAvoy not to have anything to do with her husband. He promised he would support her and her two children, providing she obtained a divorce. McAvoy was currently employed as a motion pic-

Alvin McAvoy

ture operator at a small theatre in Sacramento, California. But on the night of the derailment, McAvoy's mother was visiting him and Hecox was positive that the man had no connection with the derailment.

On August 15th, Hecox flew to New York so that he could appear on the "We The People" program which was broadcast over Columbia network. Hecox told the nation that after the tragedy, he observed one of the rails had been pried loose and pushed 4 inches from the center and spiked down. Also, he said he found a claw bar nearby, but that it was later used to rescue trapped passengers.

Regarding any employee complaint which Hecox might have registered with Southern Pacific (in the possibility that some enemy might have derailed the train to "get even"), FBI agent John Horgan interviewed John Goodfellow, the SP superintendent of the Salt Lake division in Ogden. Goodfellow said that to his knowledge Hecox had never registered any complaint against anyone.

Assistant Superintendent Thomas Foley was also questioned by Horgan. Foley had observed Hecox for the past ten years, and that to his knowledge he had never registered a complaint against

anyone. Nor, had anyone complained about the engineer.

Hecox gave a formal affidavit to O'Connell that shortly before the derailment he was studying the rails and observed a green tumbleweed lying on the track. Since tumbleweeds are dry and dead when blowing around the desert, the fact that this one was green was so unusual that he kept his eyes on it and did not notice the condition of the track ahead. He further testified that the light on the control power unit was fixed and throwing 1500 feet beams straight ahead. Hecox added that on a curve such as the one approaching and crossing the Humboldt River bridge, the bright light shines off the outside curve and hits not only the top of the outside rail, but also the inside pedestal of the outside rail. He explained that he felt a jolt when the control car went off the track immediately passing the tumbleweed. Furthermore, he found the brakes useless in trying to stop the train, although the streamliner's engines came to an abrupt stop.

Hecox explained that when he telephoned Carlin from Harney, the person answering the telephone asked him what had happened. In his excitement, he stated that the train had hit something, possibly a rock. But later he realized it would be impossible for a rock to be on the track since the road bed was on a high fill and that no rock of any size could be there unless it was placed there deliberately. He stated that his remark was probably prompted by common experiences in the past where rocks had rolled down onto road beds from high cliffs along the right-of-way.

Hecox became very indignant with the FBI suggestion that when he saw the tumbleweed on the track he thought it was a rock and applied the emergency brakes causing the train to buckle resulting in the wreck.

★   ★   ★

All those who might be suspected as having a grievance against Southern Pacific, or its officials, were checked and eliminated by O'Connell and the FBI. This phase of the investigation was to extend several months, involving the tracking down and questioning of 707 former Salt Lake division employees who were discharged or who resigned since January 1, 1938.

★   ★   ★

A week after the swimmers had started their combing of the river bed, the biggest break of the case occurred. It was during the morning of August 20th when someone burst into O'Connell's office asking him to rush down to the river. On the bank,

Photo taken at Exposition Park, Los Angeles, March, 1937.

Left to right—C. A. McDonough, J. J. Kelley, L. J. Giroux, A. K. Brennan, Wm. Gannon, D. J. Murphy, J. C. Moore, L. R. Baker, D. O'Connell, M. F. McCarthy, R. M. Jenkins, S. L. Monk, B. V. McCabe, W. R. Hayes, P. V. Herbert, D. McCoy, J. W. Rupnik.

Southern Pacific railroad detectives in 1938.

Photo taken at Arcade Passenger Station, Los Angeles, March, 1938.

Left to right—D. F. Hanley, J. W. Rupnik, E. D. Ainsworth, W. R. Hayes, A. Tarrant, J. Huber, L. R. Baker, B. V. McCabe, C. H. Dailey, J. J. Finneran, H. C. MacQueen, M. O'Connell, J. J. Kelley, C. A. McDonough, J. Downs, L. J. Giroux. On locomotive—D. O'Connell, M. F. McCarthy.

The manhunt in full swing. Possible suspects are rounded up and brought in for questioning.

124

The files of all the suspects investigated between August of 1939 and June of 1940.

a smiling diver handed him a crowbar which had been lodged against a rock under the current.

"Now we're hitting pay dirt!", exclaimed the chief. "All of you keep diving around the spot where this came from. I'll wait right here to see what you bring up. Something tells me we're on the trail."

Late that day, one of the swimmers came splashing back to shore. "Got my hands on something out there, near that big grey rock. And, it feels like cloth. Wait here. I'll have it for you in a jiffy."

What he handed to O'Connell a short time later was a man's blue zipper jacket, its sleeves tied snugly around two large rocks for weights.

"Here's what I've been waiting for!" O'Connell shouted. "This is no coincidence. Look at the way those rocks were tied in by the sleeves. Whoever did that did it to keep the jacket on the river bot-

tom. And, why was he so anxious to keep this under water?"

"Do you really think it belonged to the train wreckers?" asked the swimmer, thrilled by the importance of his discovery.

"Yes, I do, my boy," smiled the chief. "But we're not through with this river just yet. Not by a whole lot!"

O'Connell then yelled new orders to the swimmers. The diver who had found the jacket was to station himself around the spot. From that point the others were to dive in every direction. O'Connell was certain that this was only the beginning.

And he was right. It wasn't more than an hour later that another find turned up. It was a heavy sledge hammer known to railroad men as a spike maul. With difficulty, three of the divers dragged it to shore. And, to their amazement, they found a

Unloading various boxes of clues in front of the Southern Pacific building.

bulky cloth wrapped around the hammer head. Upon inspection, it turned out to be a man's tan cloth zipper jacket. The river bottom had at last yielded the vital clues necessary for careful investigation.

There was no mistaking the significance of these two finds.

"Two jackets in the river close to the bridge," O'Connell remarked to the small group of agents eyeing them that night on a table in his office. "They've been deliberately weighed down in the hope of concealing them forever. Can there be anything but one conclusion?"

All agreed that the garments must be the discarded jackets of the saboteurs. Then, the crowbar and sledge hammer were analyzed. Obviously, these were tools used in the derailment. Carefully the two coats were examined. In a pocket of the tan coat was discovered a piece of blue cloth resembling the material from which the other garment was made. The scrap of blue fabric was wrapped around a rough-edged piece of mirror. Beyond that, the pockets yielded nothing.

O'Connell rushed both jackets to FBI headquarters in Washington, D.C. While the investigation took place, divers would continue scouring the

126

river bottom. And, the very next morning, the divers uncovered a railroad track wrench close to the spot where the other tools had been found.

Soon the jackets were returned to O'Connell's headquarters and expert garment workers were called in for their advice. They noted that the tan jacket was size 38 and that it had been made of heavy Archer rubberized suede cloth with a convertible collar and two set-in slash pockets. Much of the suede finish had worn off, giving it the appearance of having been made of tan canvas.

"Here's something peculiar," said one of the ladies, pointing to a place on the back of the coat. "You'll notice that two tears have been sewed, one at the upper corner of the right pocket and the other here on the back near the left shoulder. If you look closely you'll see that the sewing has been done with what we call a 'baseball stitch,' like the stitch used in sewing together the hide covering on baseballs."

The other garmet was size 42 and fashioned from dark Navy blue Melton cloth. It had a button tab at the collar and two set-in slash pockets. The sleeves of the coat were badly worn and the back of the coat tail was missing, or as if it had been deliberately cut away. With this new information, O'Connell and his men found themselves confronted by a new task which was indeed Herculean. Before them were two coats recovered from the river's depths, found despite every effort to hide them forever.

But who and where were the men who had worn them?

★ ★ ★

Dan O'Connell (with white dot over his head) supervises unloading of vital evidence.

Exhibit boxes opened and contents displayed.

While O'Connell was in conference the next morning, FBI agent Tony Newman called him to one side and said he discovered where there had been a fire near the south side of the bridge, about a mile from the point where the wreck occurred. The fire was directly in line with the indicator signal of the track and had blazed within the last few weeks. O'Connell promptly followed Newman to the campfire site near a large boulder which was at a point about 100 yards west of the bridge's west end and about 150 yards from the river bank.

The campsite had a fireplace consisting of two rocks about eight inches apart forming a grate underneath a granite rock which was about 250 or 300 feet high. Its fire could not be observed from the track. To O'Connell, the remains of the fire appeared to be two or three weeks old. Nearby were a few pieces of wood and a small board at the base of the rock which looked as though it had been

used as a seat with the rock as a back rest. Near the fire was part of a burned tie which had nails in it marked "27." About 20 feet away was a second section of burned tie, near which was a piece of tin about 14 inches long and 12 inches wide. It appeared as if it might have been removed from some kind of a strainer, since it was perforated with several holes. Slightly bent, the tin suggested that it had been placed between two rocks as a cooking or frying device. The wood and tin pieces were rushed to Elko in an effort to obtain fingerprints. As far as O'Connell was concerned, two men had camped there for some time. Marks in the nearby embankment showed that the two had climbed to the top from which they had a clear view of the bridge and derailment site.

O'Connell now had the tools used in tampering with the track. And, it was entirely possible that he now had the campsite from which the saboteurs

could observe the coming and going of various passenger trains. Judging from the locations where the jack and tools were found, there was no doubt in O'Connell's mind that the trainwreckers followed the course of the river to the bridge, then crossed over to the Western Pacific tracks and left the railroad west of the Western Pacific tunnel heading northwest through the hills. Following this theory, O'Connell ordered several of his agents to search the tunnel hills. By late that afternoon, the footprints of two men were discovered. They were traced to a point about one mile west of Clure, a small nearby town.

★ ★ ★

Armed with this new evidence, O'Connell ordered Jim Addcox, an assistant, to investigate all the alternate roads leading to and from Clure.

With a team of Southern Pacific's best agents, and believing that the saboteurs used one of the town's routes in reaching and escaping from the scene of the derailment, Addcox went to work. The results of this top priority assignment were submitted in the following report:

SUBJECT: Rough Sketch of some of the roads in vicinity of the derailment that I checked with a view of learning how the guilty persons reached the scene of the derailment.

Road No. 1 running from Highway #40 to Palisade. Any one traveling this road would have to go thru Palisade where all the people claimed they saw no strangers on date of the derailment.

Road No. 2 leading from BuckRake Jack Ranch to Barth. Birnard Hassen who lived at Buck Jack Ranch stated that he was sitting in his yard and he

For a while, the search concentrated on this small community near Harney.

named the autos that he saw travel this road on date of derailment. These were checked out and found to be steel gang employes.

Road No. 3 leading from Palisade to the Overhead Bridge. Anyone traveling this road in auto would have likely been seen by someone in Palisade.

Road No. 4 leading from the Beowawe Road at Horseshoe ranch to WP Cluro, John Gavey, Signal Maintainer at Beowawe for the WP stated that he traveled this road at 4.00 A.M. August 13th, that there were no fresh car tracks between the Griffin Mine Road No. 5 and WP Cluro.

Road No. 6 leading from WP Cluro to Highway 40, Mr. O'Connell and myself checked this road there had been only one car over this road recently and P.S. Edler, WP Section Foreman at Cluro stated that it was him who drove over this road some few days before the derailment.

Road No. 7 leading from WP Cluro to Highway No. 40 at Twin Summits, Mr. O'Connell and myself checked this road and found that no car had been over it in months.

Road No. 8 leading from Highway No. 40 to Beowawe anyone traveling this road would have to pass thru Beowawe.

Road No. 9 leading from Beowawe to Joe Bell Ranch then thru his horse lot and in between the tracks to Harney and Cluro Mr and Mrs Bell stated that no auto traveled this road night of the derailment.

Road No. 10 leading from Beowawe around the Bell Ranch to Harney. All employes at Harney claimed they saw no auto on this road night of the derailment.

Road No. 11 leading from Beowawe via Moderelli Mine and W. H. Blairs Ranch. Moderelli Boys stated that about 1.00 P.M. August 12th, they drove from their mine to Beowawe that they had odd truck tires on their truck and that sunday Aug. 13th, they checked this road and found that there had been no vehicle of any kind from top of hill opposite the derailment to their mine since they had traveled the road the afternoon before. Mr. W.H. Blair stated that as soon as he heard of the derailment he checked this road which runs thru his horse lot and found that no auto had passed thru the night before.

Road No. 12 leading from the Beowawe to Palisade Road No. 11 to the old iron mine also leading off Road No. 13 Palisade to Frenchie Ranch road apparent was not checked by any known person before a lot of trafic passed over the road by people coming to see the wreck.

Road No. 13 leading off the Road No. 11 from Beowawe to Palisade leads to the Frenchie Ranch then beyond to Dewey Dan Ranch, Dean Ranch, Tenoba and vicinity apparently was not checked before a lot of traffic passed over it. It is possible for anyone to travel this road from Tenoba to the Iron Mine either in daytime or nighttime without being seen by any one and around this old Iron Mine is an ideal spot for anyone to have hid out even with an auto or truck either in daytime or night time without being seen.

Road No. 14 leading off the road from Beowawe to Harney just east of the Beowawe Cemetery leads to the Frenchie ranch and beyond, anyone coming in on this road would have had to turn east on roads 10 or 11 to have gotten close to the scene of the derailment.

Road No. 15 leading out of Beowawe leads to Dewey Dan's via what is known as the hot points and Road No. 16 leads from Beowawe to Tenoba, anyone coming in on either of these roads apparently would pass thru Beowawe to get to the scene of the derailment.

Road No. 17 leads from Beowawe to High Strickland Ranch and road no. 18 leads from Beowawe to Sansenini Ranch both about one mile from Beowawe any one coming from these ranches by auto would travel thur Beowawe.

It is approximately 7 miles from Highway 40 to scene of derailment, it is approximately 9 miles from Palisade to scene of the derailment, it is approximately 11 miles from Beowawe to scene of the derailment it would have been quite a distance for the guilty person or persons to have walked in

A posse returning after searching the desert for possible clues and camp sites.

Dan O'Connell (in the center) and two of his agents at Joe Bell's ranch.

from either of these points ran around and gathered up the tools used in derailing the train then walked back out after pulling the job.

It is the opinion of some of the people in the vicinity that I have interviewed that the guilty person or persons used horses to get to the scene of the derailment, horses could have been taken from the Mahoney Ranch at Dunphy, Horseshoe-ranch, Hugh Strickland, ranch, Sansenini Ranch, Joe Bell Ranch, Beowawe, W.H. Blair Ranch, Palisade and Rand Ranch, six miles up the valley from Palisade, Dewey Dan Ranch, Nean Ranch at Tenoba which are 25 miles from the scene. I have personally interviewed all these ranchers, members of their families and their hired hands and all stated that they did not hire out or loan any one

any horses on night of August 12th, 1939, and that if any of their horses were used they were stolen out by some unknown person or persons, who had returned them their barnes or pastures.

The two men's tracks found by Special Agent W.F. Boebert, that lead from the scene of the de-railment up over the hill and down to the swamp close to the W.P. Tracks just west of WP Cluro Section quarters and then were lost which would indicate that the two men might have entered an auto or rode horses out or that they might have walked west on the W.P. tracks which the later is the most like as no auto tracks or horse tracks were seen near where the tracks were lost.

If the two men making these tracks are guilty of pulling the job they were well acquainted in the vicinity for this reason, at the point where their tracks were lost they could walk the WP tracks to Beowawe without taking much chance of being seen where as if they had took the south side of the tracks they would have to dodge Harney Section, Miller Ranch, Bell Ranch, Extra Gang at SP Cluro and took a chance of being seen by people passing along the different roads.

This rough sketch that I made of a few roads in the vicinity of the derailment is not a complete map by no means as there are several roads winding around in the hills south of the tracks but the ones mentioned in the sketch are the main ones or the only roads leading into any point close to the scene of the derailment.

J.H. Addcox
Asst. Special Agent

★ ★ ★

After evaluating the report, O'Connell turned his attention back to the two jackets salvaged from the Humboldt River. How could these jackets be made to talk? Would they lead to a pair of murderers? By now, a few weeks after the sabotage, the fugitives might well be in another corner of the country. Perhaps they had even fled to some distant land. Could they be run to ground by the jackets they wore during their mass murder?

The chief and his detectives pondered these and innumerable other questions. And, the more they questioned and speculated, the more they realized the enormity of the search. But, well-trained in the methods of manhunting, O'Connell was not discouraged. To the contrary, he was elated over the discovery of such tangible clues.

"I agree that millions of men in America could fit these jackets," he told the others, "but somewhere are people who noticed them on the two men we want. There may be an innocent someone who even sewed the rips with the peculiar 'baseball stitch.' And then again . . ."

"You're sure you're not being optimistic," an agent cut in, laughingly.

"Not only am I optimistic," O'Connell chuckled, "but as you know, I am also systematic. I'd like to

Joe Bell (at the extreme left) and his daughter (center) prepare to lead Dan O'Connell and his agents to various desert sites which could have been used as camp sites.

know who sold the jackets to the wearers. But that's not the first step. If we're going to begin tracking, it's going to be in an orderly procedure. One step at a time. We've got to do it in sequence. So, our first move is to find the manufacturers of the coats. Looking for the retail stores will come later."

O'Connell went on to explain his plan. There would be a systematic checkup of every American manufacturing plant producing zipper jackets. He realized there might be thousands of such sewing concerns, but the job had to be done thoroughly. Also, he could count on the cooperation of local and federal authorities throughout the nation.

While his men busied themselves assembling a list of the hundreds of garment manufacturers,

O'Connell ordered new moves. First, he had the coats photographed. Second, he authorized the printing of thousands of circulars summarizing the crime and picturing the jackets, with a minute description of each. The circulars also announced Southern Pacific's offer of a $10,000 reward for information leading to the arrest and conviction of the owners. O'Connell's plan was to post a circular on every public bulletin board in America. They were sent to railroad depots, post offices, police stations in the largest cities as well as smallest towns, not only in the United States, but also in Mexico and Canada.

With his men undertaking this project, O'Connell began the staggering task he felt so necessary, hunting the coat manufacturers. Within a few

The group stops for lunch.

The $10,000 reward poster circulated throughout the United States, Canada, and Mexico.

Southern Pacific Company
$10,000 REWARD
Whose Jackets are These?

Description of Brown Jacket:

Man's brown or tan Cossack style zipper jacket, size 38. Made by Packard Mfgr. Co., Des Moines, Iowa, of heavy Archer rubberized suede cloth, fleece finish on inner side. Convertible collar and two set-in slash pockets. When new this jacket was seal brown in color, but when discovered by Officers the suede finish was worn off and the outside of the jacket appears as though made of tan canvas.

Description of Blue Jacket:

Man's dark Navy blue woolen zipper jacket, 33 ounce material, size 42. Made of Melton cloth, treated to repel snow and rain. It is unlined. Has button tab at collar and two set-in slash pockets. This jacket is "Hercules" brand, made for and sold by Sears Roebuck Company.

Can you give any information about the identity of the persons who wore these Jackets?

The evidence conclusively links these jackets with the persons who wrecked Southern Pacific Train No. 101, Streamliner "CITY OF SAN FRANCISCO," near Harney, Nevada, August 12, 1939, resulting in the death of 24 people and injuring 117.

The Southern Pacific Company offers a REWARD OF TEN THOUSAND DOLLARS ($10,000.00), for information leading to the arrest and conviction of the person or persons responsible for this crime.

We need the help of every law abiding person in locating those responsible for this terrible crime. You may know the man or men who wore these jackets. You may even have seen them wearing the jackets. Any information you can furnish may be valuable in aiding to bring about the arrest and conviction of the vicious criminals.

Here is the Story

About 9:35 P.M., August 12, 1939, the Streamliner "CITY OF SAN FRANCISCO" was derailed and wrecked near Harney, Nevada. This wreck was caused by some person or persons maliciously tampering with the track, on a curve near a bridge over the Humboldt River. The track spikes and angle bars connecting two rails at a joint in the track were removed by the vandals. The receiving rail of the joint was moved toward the center of the track a distance of four and five-eighths inches, then spiked to the ties in this misplaced position.

When the "CITY OF SAN FRANCISCO" reached the point where the rail had been misplaced, it was derailed. Several cars in the train struck and demolished the bridge over the Humboldt River, causing the cars and the steel bridge structure to fall into the River, bringing death and injury to a total of one hundred and forty-one persons on this train.

Help us capture those responsible for these deaths and injuries

Study the pictures of the jackets carefully. Observe how the lower part of the blue jacket has been torn. Do you remember seeing anyone wearing a jacket with the back torn in this manner? Notice the sleeves of this blue jacket; they are also torn and appear to be worn badly.

Notice the sewing at the upper corner of the right pocket, in the front view of the brown jacket. Also notice the sewing near the left shoulder, as shown in the rear view of this jacket. The stitch used is similar to that used on baseballs. Note the stitching on each sleeve of this brown jacket, from the elbows to the wrists. This is a running stitch, evenly spaced and neatly finished.

REMEMBER, THE REWARD OF TEN THOUSAND DOLLARS ($10,000.00) WILL BE PAID FOR INFORMATION LEADING TO THE ARREST AND CONVICTION OF THOSE RESPONSIBLE FOR THIS TRAIN WRECK.

Communicate any information you may have to the undersigned.

This circular supersedes previous circulars and increases the reward referred to in them to $10,000.00.

San Francisco, California, March 25, 1940.

D. O'CONNELL, Chief Special Agent,
Southern Pacific Company,
65 Market Street,
San Francisco, California.

days, the blue coat proved the easiest to trace. With the "Hercules" brand tag sewn on the back collar, it was found to have been made for and sold by the Sears Roebuck Company. But since Sears confined itself only to sales on a cash basis, it was impossible to trace its sale. Frustrated, O'Connell turned his attention to the tan jacket. Before long, he realized that the job he had undertaken was far more complex than he anticipated. His men began the tedious work of compiling a master list of the hundreds of such garment factories sprinkled throughout the United States. To railroad agents, police detectives, and other investigators went descriptions of the coat asking that the various manufacturers in their respective areas be checked individually. To thousands of other police officials, O'Connell wrote personal letters.

Slowly and laboriously the work dragged on. Week after week passed by. Then a report arrived from Washington D.C., of great importance. It was the findings of the Interstate Commerce Commission which had launched an independent and far-reaching investigation of the wreck on its own.

The commission's verdict concurred with all O'Connell's conclusions. The commission found that the derailment's site's roadbed, rails, and signals along the right of way were maintained faultlessly. Also, at the time of the tragedy, the train was within its maximum allowance of speed. The crew was cleared of any wrong doing. As far as the commission was concerned, the engineer and fireman were performing their duties meticulously. Flatly, the commission's report placed the blame on saboteurs, finding that "this accident was caused by malicious tampering with the rails."

Clearly, this was the final word of the United States government. But it did not help O'Connell and his team on the tremendous task they had undertaken, a job that was already testing their patience to the utmost. The checkup of jacket manufacturers went on, extending from one end of the nation to the other. Time and again O'Connell's spirits were raised by hopeful reports, only to have them blasted by final and more careful inquiry.

Months slipped by. Slowly, one by one, the names of manufacturers were stricken off of the master list. The process of elimination was slowly working, but without result.

Then at last came the first real breakthrough. Word was flashed to O'Connell that the tan jacket had been sewn by the Packard Manufacturing Company in Des Moines, Iowa. Company officials, however, couldn't really be positive. They insisted that an expert examination of the coat itself be made at the site of the firm. O'Connell rushed his most dependable man to Iowa with the most vital clue he had. Arriving in the company's executive office with the precious garment, a girl was called

from one of the many nearby assembly lines. She studied the suede jacket for a moment. Then, she turned to the railroad detective.

"I'm afraid I'll have to tear open the collar," she smiled. "May I have permission?"

"Yes, of course do," the agent replied.

Quickly and confidently the young woman cut open a seam joining the collar to the coat. Sure enough, there on the inner side of the material was found a number written in red crayon.

"May I now tear off the tab on the sleeve?" she asked.

Again, the agent nodded his permission.

Inside the tab was also a number scribbled in red crayon. It corresponded exactly with the number on the collar.

"Yes, there is no doubt. This coat was made here," the girl said softly with an air of finality. "We use these numbers in assembling the various parts of the garment."

The jacket was known as style 450 in the firm's wide range of different model coats.

Now, it was important to consult with production records. The company had stored away great piles of data and checking back over the records of previous years involved a tremendous task. But executives of the Packard company were eager to offer their help in every possible way they could. Quickly pulling helpers off the assembly lines, officials not only offered manpower, but also their facilities in order to dig up the necessary files.

After a few days, it was found that since 1934 when the firm began the manufacture of style 450 a total of 12,432 such jackets had been made. Of this number, 1,665 were size 38.

Because no one was exactly sure as to the size of the well-worn coat due to stretching or shrinkage in the river, O'Connell decided to track down as far as possible every single one of the 12,432 jackets of that one particular model. He wired his agent to ask for the names of all of the jobbers and retailers to whom the jackets had been sold.

When finally assembled from the factory's books, the list was nearly as voluminous as the long record of coat manufacturers that now had been traced. It included at least 8,000 stores throughout the United States. Some of them were in obscure towns and small villages. A total of 1,134 such merchants were in hamlets not even served by railroads.

O'Connell studied the list. After several moments of silence, he called in half a dozen of his most experienced men and started issuing orders.

"Every one of these dealers has to be checked, and each must be checked thoroughly. Remember how we started out blindly to find the manufacturer. That is, we were slow, deliberate, methodical, and careful. We got what we wanted by the sure process of elimination. I intend for each of you

Scrap from the wrecked cars Presidio and Mission Dolores. For convenient handling, cars were cut in sections with acetylene torch. The site is Beowawe, Nevada.

Wrecked cars loaded for shipment to Chicago.

to do the same in finding that one dealer. So, let's get moving."

Agents knew that O'Connell's grim, dogged determination was legendary. They also relized that it would take them months, perhaps even years to complete their tracking.

The enormity of the task and its incredible difficulties did not frustrate them at first. Then, as the agents became thoroughly immersed in the work before them, they slowly began to lose hope. The main reason for this was that they found themselves hindered because many of the smaller retailers sold only on a cash basis. In each instance of this kind, the agents came to the end of a blind trail, sometimes after months of tracking.

In other cases, the detectives traced customers from one state to another. Locating them at last, they would discover that they were in no way connected with the crime. In the cases of other jacket purchasers, the buyers were itinerants with no established residence. The job of tracing them proved to be more than even determined manhunters could accomplish.

Police and sheriffs in many states were called on to help in the almost endless checkup. They discovered that some dealers had retired altogether from business. Regardless, they had to be located wherever they were and their records studied.

"Nothing must interfere with this job until it's done and done thoroughly. I am absolutely determined to catch these murderers, if it's the last thing I do," O'Connell stressed to his men time and again. And, the chief special agent was going to follow through with every step of his specific and exact plan. Every dealer on his list had to be checked out, no matter how long or how much work it took.

Since the day after the derailment, O'Connell and his hand-picked staff of men maintained their headquarters at Carlin, not far from the scene of the tragedy. There he planned to remain indefinitely. For how long, he would not guess. But he swore he would remain there until the train wreckers had been caught and executed.

Occasionally, when circumstances demanded, he shuttled back to his San Francisco headquarters for a brief stay. But even there, hourly reports came to him by telephone and telegraph.

★ ★ ★

During the weeks that followed the derailment, O'Connell received daily reports from his agents in the field. Typical of one such report dated August 25, 1939, is as follows:

San Francisco, August 25, 1939.

Mr. D. O'Connell:

Referring to your D-172, date, on leads run to a conclusion; following is a list of those on which we have files:

No. 1. Robert LaDouceur, so called "earless man", arrested by Sked at Sparks, August 14 and held for investigation. Established an alibi for his whereabouts August 12. Released after questioning. You have already received information on him by wire. With this file have attached several other "tips" from various persons who reported seeing "earless men" in various parts of the Pacific Coast.

No. 2. Information from G.J. Lowen that William C. Lucas, former Section Foreman for W.P. might be guilty party. Lucas' whereabouts checked on by Matt McCourt of the Union Pacific and it was determined that he was in American Falls, Idaho, Aug. 12.

No. 3. Wire from Sam Fabrizio of the Santa Fe suggesting that William Nabors be checked, stating last they heard of him was being sentenced to McNeil Island Prison in March 10, 1937. Wired Warden at McNeil and he repled that Nabors still confined there. Also with this on Nabors attached copy of correspondence on Nabors sent us by W.G. Fetzner of the CB&Q. This was old letters from Tim O'Leary from Albuquerque dealing with Nabors' activity.

No. 4. Wire from Matt McCourt on Indian named Harry J. Missouri, picked up by his men at Salt Lake City. You checked this at Winnemucca and verified statements made by Missouri.

No. 5. Information received by Pete Casenave from officials of the State Hospital at Stockton that the wreck might be the work of Frank Rodney King, who placed obstructions on Santa Fe track near Fresno in 1937 and has since been paroled from the State Hospital. Healy checked at Fresno and determined King was in

Fresno, being seen there at 5:00 P.M. August 12, 1939.

No. 6. Sergeant McKee, California Highway Patrol, 'phoned this office August 13th, regarding unidentified drunken man seen at Hazen, August 12th, according to trespasser named W.K. Fread ejected from train at Truckee. Drunken man supposed to board Eastbound freight train about 3 PM after cursing S.P. Co. Nothing further ever heard on this and most doubtful if man could get from Hazen to Harney in time to perpetrate the wreck.

No. 7. Information from Dr. Cushman, Director of State Home at Ukiah that Kenneth Cook, former inmate released about three months ago had made threatening remarks about S.P. Co. and N.W.P. Cook and his brother convicted of robbing NWP station at Alderpoint, August 17, 1930, March Cook being sent to San Quentin and Kenneth also to San Quentin but later transferred to the Asylum account of his mental condition. Cook former extra gang laborer. Peters of N.W.P. made very close check on him and definitely placed Cook as being in Eureka on Monday, August 14th, and other information was that Cook had not been away from Eureka for some time.

No. 8. Report to this office that a Mrs. Gill, passenger on Train ahead of the Streamliner observed two men with flashlight and handcart near where Streamliner wrecked. In an interview with Investigator C.H. Dailey, Mrs. Gill stated she was on Train 87 which would pass the point of wreck between 3 and 4 PM August 12th and denied seeing anything such as reported, making signed statement to that effect. In fact, she did not know exactly where wreck did occur.

No. 9. Information from H.O. Peters that Joe Guerrero, alias Joe Gullo, ex-track-walker for NWP might be responsible. Check was made and it was developed that Guerrero is still an inmate of the State Hospital at Napa.

No. 10. Information from Peters that a man named Locatelli might be a suspect, but Peters himself made check and determined that Locatelli was in Ukiah.

No. 11. R.E. Hallawell mentioned name of R.E. Ambrose, formerly employed as machinist or electrician at West Alameda Shops where he had worked on the Streamliner, and who once worked in the Shops at

All alone in the yard.

Sparks, might be a likely suspect. Special Agent J. Prindiville and J. Eber called on Ambrose at his home in Oakland and mentioned that his troubles with the Company were his own fault, he did not appear to have any grudge and denied knowing anyone in vicinity of Harney or Beowawe. J. Prindiville feels not at all likely he had any connection.

No. 12. Van De Mark suggested check sould be made on Donald Chiniquy and Millard Fisher, particularly Chiniquy, as these were boys who did the damage at Palmdale in March, 1937. Learned that Chiniquy was paroled from the Reform School at Preston to his father and he was working with his father at the Defiance Fan Company at Los Angeles. Fisher sent to Whittier, paroled and violated and was sent to Preston. Has good record there and shortly will be eligible for reparole.

No. 13. Gust Pulos and his family were checked. Gus is still in the Alameda County Jail and his boy is working at the Westinghouse plant. Inspector Covill of the Oak-land Police Department, at request of J. Prindiville, made this check and he talked with Pulos in jail and also with Mrs. Pulos at home, not saying what his mission was. Mrs. Pulos stated it was a good thing Gus was in jail, or he would be considered responsible.

No. 14. George King, Negro attempted train wrecker checked and his presence in the Stockton State Hospital developed.

No. 15. Jesus Gutierez, who attempted to wreck a train at Decoto in 1935 was checked and he is still in San Quentin.

No. 16. Check made on E.A. O'Donnell, Houston, developed he was in Houston at time of wreck. This information given you by wire D-773, and also given Don Brown who requested result.

No. 17. Charles E. Fish. Investigation made of whereabouts and apparently he was in Los Angeles at time of wreck, according to his statement to Special Agent Tillman of F.B.I. and M.F. McCarthy. This information already furnished you.

No. 18. Information from Investigator Banich, Roseville, that former Yardmaster Bernard J. Smith, Coast Division, seen around Roseville, August 9th, apparently mentally affected and might be a suspect, as said couldn't get a job anywhere since being fired by S.P. Co. Learned he wrote J.J. Jordan letter from Barstow, August 11th and had Phillips check there, finding he went to work for Santa Fe at 6:45 A.M. August 13th, so couldn't have been at wreck.

No. 19. Man writing Mr. Dyer and also yourself, signing "The Engineer" from Box 214, Ross, Calif. Had Peters check this fellow who is William J. Flynn. He had theory that the wreck was caused by the bridge giving away from the high waters of Humboldt River undermining it. He has had no training as an engineer and likes to talk on all subjects.

No. 20. L.R. Smith called attention of J. Prindiville to William Wilder, who burned the bridge at Byron. Check at Stockton State Hospital showed he was still there.

No. 21. Letter from R. J. Edgeworth giving copies of statements taken by his Officers from Roscoe Anthony, who was in LaSalle St. Station Chicago, August 14, and spoke of terrible wreck and said railroads would continue to have wrecks if they threw men off trains like they did on the Seaboard Air

The Twin Peaks damaged beyond repair.

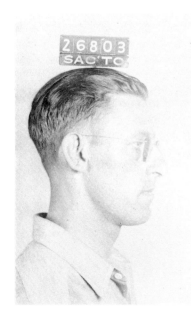

William Van Volkenburg

Line until they wrecked some trains on them. From statements taken Anthony apparently a little unbalanced mentally and had no money, so could very unlikely have been at the wreck August 12th and be in LaSalle St. Station on August 14.

No. 22. Mention by Mr. Fred Howard of Roger Grady, former rate clerk. This sent out to you and D. Quillinan made notation that learned Grady recently taken to City and County Hospital with stomach ulcers and is in serious condition.

No. 23. General Manager's office staff mentioned former employee named Shelley, who called at General office August 17th and wanted to see Mr. Dyer. He is also going to sue the company about something. He is an elderly man, about 70, admitted to practice law. Hayes interviewed him in Los Angeles, where he lives, under pretext and he stated positively was in Los Angeles on August 11th and 12th. He is a letter writer.

No. 24. Mrs. Nairn, 1779 - 85 Ave., Oakland reported that about August 10 or 11th a man representing Sherman Clay & Co. called at her home and she had conversation with him during which he stated he and another man worked on design of a streamline train, but lost all their money in it and that different railroad engineers came to their plant while they were working on the model, and soon afterward he learned the first streamline train was built. Herbert made the check and stated no connection between this man and the accident.

No. 25. Inspector Covill, Oakland Police, reported to J. Prindiville that un-named investment broker advised him a man called on him in June or July and in conversation man spoke bitterly about the railroads, but no particular railroad mentioned. That the man stated he would soon hear of one of the biggest railroad wrecks in the history of the country. According to Covill, the broker did not recall the man's name or where he could be located or anything about him, but promised if he did hear from the man again or could get information as to who he was, the broker would inform Covill. Nothing further has been heard on this.

No. 26. Letter from J.J. Brennan of the Santa Fe regarding one Josiah F. Hobart, who confessed wrecking D&RGW train but nothing could be learned on it. Peters checked near Fortuna, where he formerly lived, and got an address in Pacific Grove and check was made there, showing J.F. Hobart and his father had recently gone to Branscomb, Calif., to act as caretakers at a place called Wilderness Lodge. Peters checked there yesterday and found Hobart and his father were there at time of wreck and have now gone to Pacific Grove again. Hobart is eccentric, apparently from self abuse.

A.J. McKenna

Among O'Connell's duties was the arrest and conviction of William Van Volkenburg who arrived on the scene the morning following the derailment dressed in the uniform of a deputy sheriff. While snooping around, he was observed by a passenger lifting a necklace from the body of a passenger. Admonished that he had no right to do that since a coroner was nearby, the imposter promptly stuffed the necklace into his pocket and fled.

O'Connell's agents quickly learned his name and followed him. They observed Van Volkenburg give the necklace to the wife of a police officer that afternoon in Elko, asking her to keep it for him. He was promptly arrested and the necklace returned to the coroner.

O'Connell's personal log from this trying and difficult period indicates that every single tip or other piece of information was investigated thoroughly. As far as he was concerned, everyone was liable to suspicion, from mid-western Nazi-Bund sympathizers to the simplest hobos.

★   ★   ★

In December of that year, Eugene Block, a nationally known mystery writer who published in such magazines as "True Detective," was instructed by his editor-in-chief in New York to check on the progress of O'Connell's manhunt, as well as to offer the magazine's assistance in blanketing the country with new reward circulars in future issues.

After several days of patient waiting, Block was notified to meet O'Connell in his office at the Southern Pacific building located on San Francisco's lower Market Street. Block found O'Connell buried in a small mountain of papers piled high on his desk. The chief special agent glanced up at him, meeting his greeting with a friendly nod. But O'Connell had little time for conversation.

"Only here for a few hours," he said almost apologetically. "I have to get right back to Nevada."

Block studied the tall, handsome, muscular figure. In his trim dress of banker's grey, he could

The battered sides of the dormitory car and the Market Street.

have passed for a man of business or finance. In reality, he was the chief of a far-flung police department which covered much of the western slope, extending through California into Utah, Texas, and New Mexico.

Block recalled stories O'Connell had told him years before during more leisurely hours. The writer saw him tracking over desert lands or through narrow passes, fearlessly leading posses in the hunt for train robbers of earlier days. Block could envision him combing the Oregon mountain vastness for clues resulting in the world famous capture of the celebrated D'Autremonts. And, he saw him again courageously capturing Roy Gardner, California's nicest badman, the Houdini of American jails.

Now, Block saw O'Connell following the scent of two men who once wore zipper jackets. They would be his prize catch, the culmination of a career as a railroad detective. Absorbed in his job, the agent was now checking reports which were coming in from far and wide. Drumming his pencil, he turned in his desk and looked down upon the rumbling traffic of Market Street. Then, he fixed his eyes on the Ferry Building towering near by. Occasionally, he would look up and smile at Block. "This man with greying hair and high forehead has deep, penetrating eyes. Those eyes speak of the unswerving determination of a seasoned manhunter," reflected Block.

O'Connell was delighted to know that "True Detective" would publish pictures of the jackets in all their future issues. Coupled with the 177,000 circulars bearing the pictures and descriptions of the jackets which had already been distributed, the new publicity would reach an additional 50,000 people.

★   ★   ★

By the beginning of 1940, Dan O'Connell had received a number of tips which suggested exconvicts, or persons with prior criminal associations, as likely suspects who might want to derail the streamliner for purposes of robbing the dead.

However, most of these leads showed that the suspected persons were in prison or jail at the time of the sabotage. In the course of tracing all these men, O'Connell made it routine to check on their known friends and associates.

While doubts were expressed concerning the ability of a psychotic or mentally deranged person to formulate and carry out all the details necessary for such a well-planned derailment, O'Connell knew from experience that in many instances trains had indeed been wrecked by the demented. And, not only could such a person plan and execute this kind of mass murder, but he generally escaped from the scene without detection.

In July of 1939, O'Connell was cooperating with railroad detectives from the Great Northern Railway in the search for a man known as Albert Fry, a former inmate of the Washington State Insane Hospital. Fry was being sought for questioning in connection with an attempt to wreck a freight train on the Great Northern. When the City of San Francisco was sabotaged, O'Connell redoubled his efforts to find Fry, distributing his photograph and description to all the police agencies in the United States. In several instances, hobos who saw the

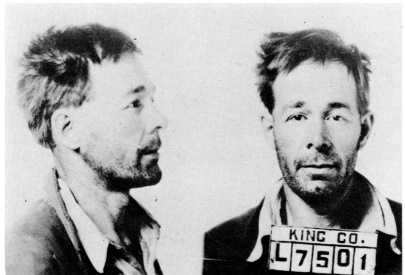

Albert Fry

photograph identified Fry as being the trespasser they had spotted on Southern Pacific rights of way, or beating his way on SP freight trains.

Though each bit of information which seemed to develop Fry's whereabouts was carefully followed to a conclusion, Fry was never apprehended. A notation was then placed on his fingerprint record in the National Bureau of Identification in Wash-ington, D.C., that he was wanted for questioning regarding the derailment.

★ ★ ★

In January, the following editorial appeared in the Red Bluff, California, "NEWS." Entitled "Keep Your Confidence," it was typical of other

Ready for shipment to Chicago.

editorial comments and letters-to-the-editor appearing throughout the country.

KEEP YOUR CONFIDENCE

Do not let the Nevada train wreck undermine your confidence in railroads. The wreck was not the fault of the Southern Pacific management or any member of the crew. The railroad uses every modern device and the train that was wrecked was constructed of the best possible materials. Had old-fashioned wooden coaches made up that train, few would have survived.

The disaster was due to a maniac. The Nevada peace officers and the railroad could not possibly have thwarted his scheme except by accidently finding him on the rail. The maniac might have caused as many deaths by other means, such as setting fire to a building in which many were sleeping, undermining the foundation of a bridge carrying heavy traffic or running wild with a gun on a busy street.

The Southern Pacific, operated by a loyal and efficient group of Americans, remains one of the safest means of transportation, serving through summer's heat and winter's storms, a great section of the United States.

★ ★ ★

By the end of January, 362 major tips had been received. During the investigation of those tips, 1,846 people had been interviewed. When each investigative report was received, O'Connell personally checked it out, always keeping in mind possible motives. If he felt that more data on the activities, background, and movements of the suspect might be of value, he immediately dispatched a special agent to investigate.

Since the beginning of the manhunt there had been 51 arrests. The lists of the arrested showed they were not confined to any particular geographic area. FBI laboratory comparisons were made between specimens of the suspect's hair and samples of human hair found on the jackets. FBI technicians said that the two jackets held strands of light golden brown hair of a "somewhat unusual type." Any suspect who had light brown hair was automatically detained and investigated thoroughly. But none of the suspects' hair matched the specimens obtained from the jackets.

O'Connell learned early in his career that underworld figures often receive valuable information about various crimes which they will not voluntarily divulge to the police. But, if properly approached, they might furnish some lead or tip that could be of value. With this thought in mind, O'Connell ordered that a canvass be made of the different gambling spots, as well as houses of prostitution between Elko and Reno. The gamblers, bartenders, prostitutes, brothel keepers, and their consorts were contacted and politely asked to furnish any information they had, or might obtain in the future.

Special agents immediately called their attention to the $10,000 reward offered by Southern Pacific for information leading to the arrest of the train wreckers. They were promised the reward would be paid promptly should arrests be made. When this was discussed with them, most remarked that in their opinion the $10,000 was insufficient to bring forth the needed information. The case was much too important for such a paltry sum. Several felt a reward of $50,000, or even $25,000, would be more in line with the viciousness of the mass murder. Remarks of this kind were echoed by more respected Nevada citizens.

While the search of brothels and gambling houses was not productive, O'Connell was glad that he had made such a check. His feeling was that a future chance remark might be made within earshot of one of these people, and with their cupidity having been aroused by the reward offered, new information might come forth.

On February 5th, O'Connell addressed a letter to the chief special agents of all 140 railroads in the U.S. and Canada. He summarized the case's modus operandi, jackets recovered, and footprints found near the spot where the "earless man" disappeared. Those footprints bore the imprint of a "Ritz" brand heel. O'Connell asked that the officers continue the lookout for any person wearing similar jackets, or shoes with this brand of rubber heel. In addition, he requested that each railroad furnish him with any information it had in its files concerning sabotage of a similar nature.

In response to this letter, he received data on 23 major cases of train wrecking. Each file sent him by the other train companies was closely checked. In those cases where arrests were made and convictions obtained, or even where suspects were mentioned though not convicted, O'Connell made every effort to locate the whereabouts of the suspects.

In mid-February when the FBI submitted its final report dealing with their participation in the case, it included under various subheadings 89 suggestions for further inquiry. O'Connell made a note of each suggestion and compared it with the data contained in his own files. He found that 23 of the FBI suggestions had already been investigated either completely or in part by his men. The remaining 65 suggestions would promptly be followed up.

The most important suggestion made in the FBI report was that further efforts be devoted toward locating the retailer of the tan jacket recovered from the Humboldt River. Through laboratory tests, it was definitely proven that the person who wore the tan colored jacket participated in the derailment. The paint stains on the jacket were exactly the same as those on the misalined rail.

While the FBI made checks on the El-Kay brand enamel with which the rail had been painted, O'Connell and his staff theorized that the Woolworth store in Ogden, Utah, was the most likely place for the train wreckers to have bought the special enamel. It was learned that shipments of the paint's brand and color were made to that store in April and July of 1939. Though it could not be positively determined by the store's manager in which of the two months the shipment of the enamel arrived, cans of such paint bearing the identical code number of the enamel used in painting the track were found on his sales shelves.

O'Connell immediately interviewed all the clerks who worked at the paint counter. Though several recall making sales of this type enamel, none could describe the persons to whom the paint had been sold.

The jackets were then shown to various sales girls and one of them claimed that some time during that summer she had seen a man walking through the store wearing such a blue zipper jacket. The tail of the jacket had been cut in the same way as the back of the blue jacket recovered from the stream. However, the woman could not recall other tears in the blue jacket. She said that she called the attention of another sales girl to the man wearing the jacket because it was so unusual. When the second girl was interviewed, she easily recalled the incident. But she could not remember the exact time of the year it occurred, nor could she describe the man wearing the jacket. Both girls felt the man with the blue jacket did not buy any paint.

Another salesgirl said that during the summer while working at the paint counter, she noticed a man standing nearby wearing a tan jacket. She particularly remembered this man because he seemed to be waiting for someone and not making any purchases himself. She could not describe him other than that he seemed to be a transient and that there was a long tear on one sleeve of his jacket near the shoulder. She could not recall which sleeve was torn, nor the approximate length

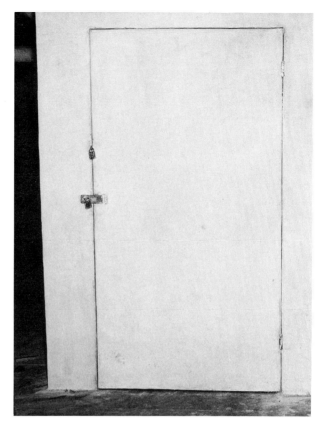

The storeroom where the evidence was placed. It is still located in the basement of the Southern Pacific headquarters in San Francisco. All the evidence remains intact.

of the tear. She says she remembered him because it struck her that he should be buying needles and thread at the notions counter rather than just loitering around the store near the paint counter.

★　★　★

O'Connell next turned his attention to the ten active mines scattered at various distances from the derailment site. Along with these, agents began scrutinizing the eleven ranches and four sheep camps nearby. In addition, numerous abandoned mines and prospect holes, as well as deserted cattle and sheep camps were carefully searched.

O'Connell then arranged to have photographs made showing in detail the markings of the tools found in the river. His hope was that information might be secured in terms of where the tools used in perpetrating the derailment had come from. Some had been stolen from a metal chest belonging

The rear of the baggage-dormitory car and the front end of
the Market Street.

to the section gang assigned to the Harney rails. But where had the larger tools come from? Their pictures were displayed to various employees of the Salt Lake division. A further check of tool houses along the various railroad lines was made in an effort to locate tools bearing similar markings. Officers soon found one or more tools bearing similar markings among the tool supplies of several section gangs. However, no one from the section gangs could make a definite statement that the spike maul, track wrench, and claw bar were part of the tool supplies of his particular gang.

At the end of February, O'Connell submitted a report to the president of Southern Pacific summarizing the investigation to date:

	Interviews to date
Investigation of 362 clues	1,846
Employees, Carlin and vicinity	688
Residents, Carlin, Beowawe, and Palisade	746
Checking former claimants	80
Checking mental patients	52
Photos of jackets displayed to	8,201
Spike maul and jackets shown to	594
Former Salt Lake Division	
employees located	510
Checking inquiries suggested by the F.B.I.	533
TOTAL INTERVIEWS	13,250

Trespassers ejected and questioned, names and addresses obtained:	41,205
Trespassers arrested and questioned, names and addresses obtained:	943
Trespassers ejected and questioned, names and addresses not obtained:	37,712
TOTAL	79,890

GRAND TOTAL OF PERSONS INTERVIEWED BY OUR OFFICERS REGARDING WRECK, AUGUST 12, 1939 to FEBRUARY 30, 1940   93,110

★ ★ ★

On Tuesday evening, March 3rd, the telephone rang in O'Connell's makeshift desert office. He had just put on his scarf and overcoat to walk back to his hotel room for a night's rest. It was Sheriff Alan Johnson of Susanville, California, who said he had a man by the name of Clarence Alexander in custody. The man had just confessed to being the saboteur. Johnson said that as far as he could determine, the 24 year old Oklahoma itinerant's account of how he wrecked the streamliner in order to rob dead passengers during the confusion checked "to the smallest detail." Said the sheriff, "I am convinced that the confession is true and that his motive, as he says, was solely one of robbery."

Clarence Alexander, 24 year old Oklahoma itinerant, confessed he had derailed the streamliner. Note how the jacket recovered from the Humboldt River fit perfectly.

Although dubious, O'Connell immediately ordered a car be made available. After calling SP headquarters in San Francisco, he and several aides departed Nevada for Susanville.

Early the next morning in Susanville, O'Connell learned that Alexander was an army deserter who had just been arrested for hit and run driving with a stolen motorcycle. During questioning in the county jail by the sheriff, he suddenly blurted out a confession.

That afternoon he was taken by O'Connell in a private plane to the scene of the derailment. O'Connell, Johnson, and other agents and deputies went over the scene thoroughly with him. Although various points in his confession tallied with the known evidence, it was obvious that the information had come from newspaper sources.

Alexander insisted he was the saboteur and that he acted alone. However, when he attempted to demonstrate how he moved the rail, he became hopelessly confused. The demented fellow did not know how to handle the necessary equipment.

Deeply disappointed that they did not have the real murderer, Johnson and O'Connell were forced to release Alexander after a thorough check was made of his whereabouts during the night of August 12th.

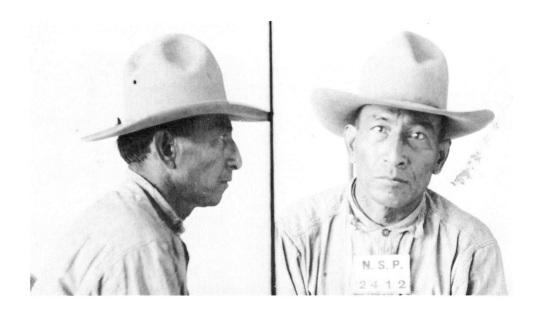

Billy Bill

* * *

In the middle of March, O'Connell's attention once again turned toward Hecox as the possible cause of the derailment.

While checking memoranda of file in the Southern Pacific office in Carlin, G.V. Dierst discovered a letter to V.L. Arcega, special agent for the SP, in which a Mrs. Benoist said that Hecox had been receiving threatening letters from an ex-convict, and that the engineer had in turn been corresponding with the man. The FBI was immediately asked to help investigate this startling new lead.

When questioned, Hecox explained that the year before the Reno "GAZETTE" carried an article on his earlier life which mentioned that he had been a stage coach driver. A short time later, a man by the name of Ernest Tatie, an inmate at Folsom Prison in California, wrote to Hecox that he had once worked along side of him.

Hecox told the FBI that he and Tatie exchanged a few pleasant letters recalling the early days, but that he was positive that Tatie was still in prison. The engineer also explained that he could not recall Tatie, although it was entirely possible he had known him fifty years before.

Dierst asked the SP veteran whether he knew anyone who might have wanted to enter his cab on the streamliner. Hecox answered that he never had any trouble of this type. He added, however, that ten years before he had thrown some youngsters off his locomotive when they boarded it in Imlay, Nevada. At that time, the engine was taking on water. Hecox chuckled as he explained that these were the only kinds of trouble he had ever experienced in all his service of railroading.

Somehow, O'Connell, Dierst, and the FBI agents were not entirely satisfied with the engineer's casualness. Also, it had long been known among SP personnel that Hecox was a "lady's man." It could be possible that a disgruntled husband tried to kill him. Yet, after careful review of his confidential records and secret FBI investigations conducted on him, not one scrap of evidence turned up linking him with the derailment.

* * *

By April, a report reached O'Connell that certain members of the Palisade community had been bitter toward railroads in general since the Eureka Nevada Railway discontinued its operation in the area a few years before. Because of this, Southern Pacific had to close the station in Palisade, causing 20 or more of the residents to lose their jobs. Each one of these individuals had to be thoroughly investigated.

Also, a report reached O'Connell of the disappearance of an old Indian named Billy Bill. Well known in the area, Billy had lived alone in a shack near the derailment site. There was speculation that the fellow might have seen the saboteurs and therefore murdered.

O'Connell instructed an agent to investigate immediately. But the search was hampered because of the snow on the hills. Not only had Billy disappeared, but so had his horse, goat, and sheep. Searching his cabin a while later, the agent found that his winter clothing and bedding were still intact. The signs were ominous.

Dan O'Connell and several of his railroad detectives in 1929.

Another major lead O'Connell pursued concerned Harry Hawkins, a 20 year SP section hand living in Palisade. Fired a few years before due to mental deficiency, the man carried a grudge against the company. But after checking this tip out, it was learned the man had not worked in the vicinity for eleven months. Living in Eureka, Nevada, about 90 miles south of Palisade, Hawkins was currently working for the Works Progress Administration.

Because new leads such as these were cropping up all the time, O'Connell assigned Alan Pfaendler to remain permanently in Palisade. Although the agent remained on duty from March, 1940, through April, 1941, nothing sufficant turned up.

★　★　★

Many of the tips O'Connell received were the result of informers hoping to discredit the reputa-tions of the accused. At first glance, many of the leads appeared to be reasonable. But Dan was most sensitive in refraining from taking any action which might reflect upon the character of the person being investigated.

Indeed, on a number of occasions, the "tips" were so fantastic that they served as humorous stimulants for the morale of those relentlessly engaged in the deadly serious investigation.

★　★　★

On May 8th, O'Connell received information that a rancher was accusing Southern Pacific of deliberately falsifying the "accident" so that it would appear as an act of sabotage. The man was telling anyone who would stop and listen that on the night of the derailment he observed railroad employees under one of the cars pounding spikes into a tie. Joe Bell who owned a ranch adjoining

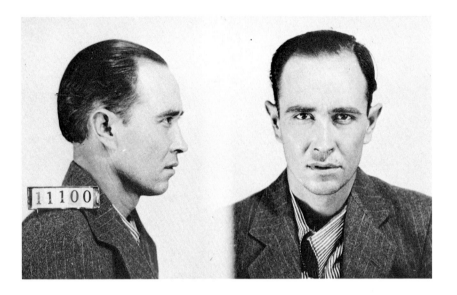

Andrew Wallace

the Southern Pacific right of way near Harney felt the wreck occurred because of excessive speed. Two of his sons who were with him also heard the pounding on the misalined rail and its tie. O'Connell immediately dispatched several agents to investigate.

★   ★   ★

Billy Bill, the old Indian who mysteriously disappeared prior to the derailment, showed up at the home of Willie Cortez in Carlin on the night of May 19th. O'Connell happened to be nearby checking out another lead at the time. He arranged for Cortez to bring Billy to Elko for questioning by Jack Gibson, a chief of the Shoshone tribe. Notified in advance of the kind of information O'Connell wanted, Gibson eagerly aided in the questioning.

Billy explained that the reason he left the area was because Ted Hawkins, the brother of Harry Hawkins, arrived at his cabin several times in July under the influence of alcohol and accused the old fellow of stealing a horse. He threatened to have Bill thrown in jail. Bill also heard gun shots several times that night and believed that Hawkins was determined to kill him. Terrified, he turned his sheep loose and took his horse and goat to an abandoned mine about 25 miles north of Carlin where he spent the entire winter. Subsisting on cotton tails and jack rabbits, Billy did not come in contact with a single human being during the entire time. He trapped eight wild cats and brought their pelts to Cortez who might sell them for him.

Bill was questioned at length as to any suspicious characters he may have seen, or anything of a suspicious nature he may have observed in the canyon west of Palisade. He said he had not observed anyone or noticed any footprints in the vicinity.

O'Connell was satisfied that if Billy Bill had any information, he would pass it on to Gibson, since the chief was loved by all the Indians in the area for championing the cause of the Shoshones. Billy was assured that a call would be made to the sheriff and that the old fellow would not have any more trouble with Hawkins. But the old fellow insisted he would never return to Palisade. In the future, he would live in an isolated cabin owned by his friend Willie Cortez.

★   ★   ★

Within a week of the derailment, O'Connell had permanently assigned 30 of his best detectives to the case. The FBI added a further six agents. Now, in January of 1941, only five railroad detectives and one FBI agent remained on the case. However, at one point or other during the investigation, practically every one of Southern Pacific's 550 agents had been assigned to duty on the sabotage. The only case in western railroad history which could be compared to the present investigation was the DeAutremont case. In that instance, train robbers dynamited a mail car, killing four men in the process. O'Connell knew the identity of the criminals from evidence left behind. But it took four years of worldwide search using every investigative facility of the federal government to capture the three DeAutremont brothers. Southern Pacific alone spent $75,000 while the U.S. government poured in over three times that amount. Two and a half million circulars printed in six languages were distributed throughout the world.

Summary of the Search Through December, 1940	
Major clues investigated	536
Persons interviewed while investigating clues	2,607
Suspects arrested	97
Wanted notices filed by the FBI	29
Ex-convicts investigated	137
Former employees located and questioned	536
Demented persons investigated	106
Former claimants checked	165
Firms checked for Style 450 jacket sales	191
New reward circulars distributed	85,364
Trespassers ejected and questioned, names and addresses obtained	84,863
Trespassers ejected and questioned, names and addresses not obtained	87,770

★   ★   ★

In early February of 1941, a prostitute named Shirley Anderson was sitting in a bar in San Jose, California, watching a Southern Pacific agent post a reward circular on the wall. Casually, she mentioned she had worked in various "houses" all over Nevada. While in Mountain City, Nevada, during the latter part of 1939, she met a man whose name was Andrew Jackson. He boasted he knew who derailed the streamliner.

Within days, O'Connell learned that the man was Andrew Jackson Wallace. Although he had left Mountain City, he was traced to Atlanta, Idaho, and placed under arrest. When questioned, Wallace explained that three months prior to the derailment he was standing in front of the Buckhorn Bar in Winnemucca, Nevada, with a fellow named Holland. As the City of San Francisco cruised by, Holland commented, "Wouldn't that train look pretty wrecked?" Since Holland was an older man, Wallace didn't pay much attention to the remark.

Efforts were immediately launched to locate Holland. Upon obtaining his photograph from the FBI, O'Connell discovered he was the same man who was arrested in 1929 as a suspect in the attempted derailment of a train near Ming, Arizona. At that time, O'Connell had obtained information from two transients that Holland had been talking of "throwing switches" and robbing a passenger train after everyone was killed. It was over a year later that Holland was arrested. And, that arrest took place in San Francisco quite by accident when he and two partners were picked up as a team of bad check writers. After questioning the man for over a week, O'Connell was forced to admit that he had no evidence whatsoever to detain him. Hol-

Holland is in the center after an arrest in San Francisco two years after the derailment.

land's photograph was shown to everyone between Winnemucca and Elko, but no one could identify him as having been in the vicinity at the time of the derailment.

★   ★   ★

After reading a reward circular, Martin Sanchez, a retired section laborer living in San Pablo, California, recalled a threat he overheard as a patient in the Southern Pacific hospital back in October of 1937. He said that a Mexican who was injured while carrying a switch stand in Elko remarked, "If the company doesn't pay me for getting hurt, I'll wreck the streamliner and put it in the Humboldt River. There is a bridge there and nothing will be left."

O'Connell learned the man was Rosalio Quintero, a section laborer, who was injured at Toy, Nevada, on July 30th, 1937. He was in the hospital for a year and received a settlement of $625. However, on the date of the derailment he was working at Lovelock, Nevada, about 170 miles west of the scene of the tragedy. After quitting work that evening he sent a registered letter to his brother in Los Angeles. O'Connell felt that if he were bitter toward the company and planned sabotaging the City of San Francisco, he might give his brother some hint of it in the letter. The brother was contacted in Los Angeles and the letter retrieved. But it proved to be a reply to a personal question the brother had asked Rosalio about and nothing more.

Rosalio Quintero

*   *   *

A week later, O'Connell received an anonymous letter with a return address of "Box 182, Ruth, Nevada" suggesting that two men in Ely, Nevada, should be considered prime suspects. One of the men was the brother of a prostitute. The writer also suggested that a member of the FBI assist in the investigation.

Within hours, the anonymous writer was identified as Herbert Wilson. Agents quickly learned that the man had a grievance against the two fellows because one of them had beaten up his friend.

Mervin Amick and Earl Coleman were picked up in Ely's red light district and taken to the sheriff's office for questioning. They furnished statements of their whereabouts on the date of the derailment. An immediate check eliminated them. The sheriff, however, severely reprimanded them for living on the earnings of a prostitute since they admitted Amick's sister was supporting them. The two were ordered to leave town.

*   *   *

Charles Pilkington, Chief Special Agent of the Cotton Belt Route, telephoned O'Connell that one of his freight trains had been wrecked near Winfield, Texas, in April of 1932. A switch had been maliciously tampered with. He strongly suspected a discharged section laborer named A.W. Sanders and his step-son, Bill Herron. But Pilkington could not obtain conclusive evidence. However, while the investigation was in progress, the two murdered a sheriff in Winfield and were

sent to prison. Sanders died in prison and Herron was released in June of 1937. Pilkington felt Herron was so vindicative that he might well be the train wrecker.

After extensive investigation, O'Connell learned that Herron had been living quietly near Fleetwood, Oklahoma. On the day of the derailment, the man was working on a farm.

*   *   *

In addition to these false leads, O'Connell and his staff investigated 81 other leads under the broad catagory "Suggested Further Inquiries." All the information O'Connell received that year could be divided into four main groups:

(1) Tips from persons who actually believed they saw individuals wearing one, or both, of the jackets depicted on the reward notice;

(2) Letters, telegrams, postcards, etc., from parties whose communications were definitely those of the perverted type;

(3) Communications from those who mistakenly believed they saw the jackets since the date of the derailment;

(4) Attempts by various men to convince O'Connell they possessed secret information, or methods which would enable them to capture the saboteurs, if Southern Pacific were willing to employ them as detectives.

*   *   *

In mid-March of 1941, the first lawsuit against Southern Pacific by injured passengers aboard the ill-fated streamliner was heard before U.S. Dis-

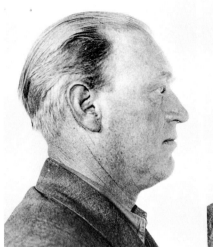

Bill Herron, alias Darrell King

trict Judge A. F. St. Sure in the southern division of the U.S. District Court in San Francisco. The plaintiffs, Eleanor and Harry Wallor, were seeking to recover damages resulting from their injuries due to Southern Pacific's negligence. The case was to be tried in a court without a jury.

The complaint stated that Southern Pacific and its agent (engineer Hecox)

"so negligently and carelessly managed, operated, used, and maintained said line of railroad, and negligently allowed the same and its appliances to be and remain unsafe and defective, and so negligently and carelessly managed, used and operated its trains, and did so carelessly and negligently and unskillfully conduct the running and operation of said train, that, for want of due care and attention

to their duties in that behalf, the passenger car in which plaintiffs were riding as passengers, was negligently allowed and permitted by the defendants to run off the track of said railroad and be derailed, while said train was running at a high rate of speed, and said car, by reason of the negligence and carelessness of defendants while being run and operated as aforesaid after being derailed did upset, was thrown down an embankment and plaintiffs were violently thrown against the sides of the car and hurt. . ."

The case was going to be tried on the theory of "res ipsa loquitur." That is,

"In the Plaintiffs' opinion, res ipsa loquitur means that the facts of the occurrence warrant the inference of negligence, not that they

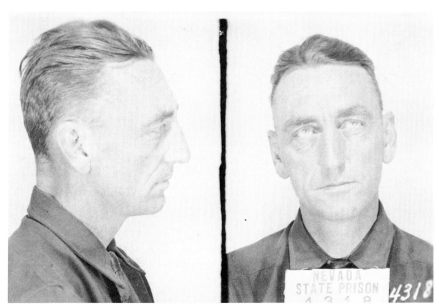

A.W. Sanders, alias William Armstrong

compel such an inference; that they furnish circumstantial evidence of negligence where direct evidence to be weighed, not necessarily to be accepted as sufficient; that they call for explanation or rebuttal, not necessarily that they require it; that they make a case to be decided by the jury, not that they forestall the verdict. Res ipsa loquitur, where it applies, does not convert the defendant's general issue into an affirmative defense. When all the evidence is in, the question for the jury is, whether the preponderance is with the plaintiff. Such, we think, is the view generally taken of the matter in well-considered judicial opinions such as Sweeney v. Erving, 228 U.S. 233, 240. . ."

The plaintiffs rested upon a prima facie showing that the defendants account for the accident.

Naturally, Southern Pacific's theory was that the "accident" was caused by vandalism and not by any agency or agent under its control.

During the course of the trial, evidence in great detail was presented showing the construction and operation of the train, the train movement between Ogden and Sparks, the physical characteristics of the country, and detailed information on the track, curve 613, and bridge no. 4.

The evidence gathered by the ICC and the FBI supported Southern Pacific's contention that the disaster was an act of sabotage. Therefore, the doctrine of res ipsa loquitur no longer applied, especially when there was specific evidence there was intervention by a third party.

But the Wallors argued that the evidence of derailment was fabricated by employees of the railroad after the accident. However, no direct charge of venality was made. On the other hand, Southern Pacific lawyers urged that the evidence was susceptible of such an inference, as well as that of sabotage. If the facts were consistent with either of two opposing theories, neither could be proven. In such an event, "judgment must go against the

Joe Bell and his family.

party upon whom rests the necessity of sustaining one of these inferences as against the other."

In rebuttal, the Wallors offered the testimony of rancher Joe Bell. On the night of the derailment, Bell hurried from a dance to the scene of the derailment. He testified,

"Well, we came over the hill and we could see fires burning. They were bonfires. There wasn't a sound. You could see people standing around the fires. When we got closer to the fires and the tracks, we could hear some pounding, like pounding on iron or some kind of metal being pounded into wood. I didn't think much of it. But later, I thought how strange the pounding was since it came from toward the back end of the train, the east end of the bridge. Me and my son went back to see what was going on. When we got there, I saw Bianchini, or Bianchini's twin brother, sitting right in the middle of the track, or on the rails, with his back kind of sideways to me. You know he works for the SP. Well, around him were two or three other SP workers. I can't say just which. They were sitting there or kneeling. Although we watched them for 10 to 20 seconds, I saw them working at something very hard. But I can't tell you exactly what they were doing. Anyway, we turned away since they were busy and didn't want to be bothered. We headed across the stream to help those who needed aid."

Twelve year old Joe Bell, Jr., who accompanied his dad, testified that when he approached the wreck he also heard and saw the pounding, but that he wasn't positive as to what was going on.

On the witness stand next, Joseph Bianchini, who was a section foreman for the Southern Pacific living in Harney, said under oath that he had been awakened by Hecox at about 10:00 p.m. and told of the derailment. He quickly assembled his gang. After Hecox reported the event by telephone to the train dispatcher, they all went back by track motor car to the scene of the disaster. Immediately upon arrival, Bianchini sent Fogus back to Harney where a further report was telephoned to Southern Pacific headquarters in San Francisco. While his gang were aiding in the rescue operations, he examined the displaced rail. It was at this time that Bell arrived and saw him under the Union Square car. But he swore he had not been pounding upon anything.

Southern Pacific lawyers concluded that

"The testimony offered to support the theory that the evidence of derailment was manufactured after the wreck by employees of defendant railroad company is wholly insufficient and insubstantial. A suggestion so incredible cannot be sustained against the indisputable physical facts and testimony of unimpeached witnesses to the contrary."

The lawyers then called several witnesses in surrebuttal. Mrs. L.E. Deiley was a passenger in the berth car Golden Gate, sixth from the end of the train. About ten minutes after the train derailed, she climbed out and walked to the east embankment of the river where a large bonfire was burning. This was at the point where the train had parted and the bridge destroyed. The car Union Square beneath which the displaced rail was discovered was about two car-lengths distant. There was a second bonfire on the fill about a car-length distant from the point of derailment. She was in the vicinity with other passengers until 3:00 a.m. She saw all the conditions under the Union Square. She testified,

"There were men on the north side, no, wait a minute — on the *south* side of the track. There were men under the car with lights. They weren't under the car directly, but to one side, and the north side of the car was perfectly free, so I could see from that side that the rail had been pushed over against the north rail. I could tell that the tie plate had been removed and respiked. On the north side of the tie plate were two spikes that were out four or five inches. They were that high. They weren't pounded all the way in as is usually done. The other two on the south side were clear in, more down like. At no time did I hear any pounding going on under the car and I stayed nearby for the entire night. At no time did I receive an impression that men were trying to cover up the derailment to look like an act of sabotage. From what I saw, it was a simple case of someone deliberately wrecking the train by pushing the rail over."

Edmund Becker was the next to take the witness stand. He had been a passenger in the car Seal Rock, fifth from the rear end west of the Union Square. After the derailment, he glanced at his watch and remained indoors. Then he stepped down to the ground and noted it was 10:05 p.m. He walked to the edge of the river where the bridge was a shambles. A bonfire had been started. Becker said,

"I spent practically all of my time around there. Right around the outside of the car, back and forth along the side of the train. We were there and around there all night, until the early morning, when the last three cars of the part of the train were taken away. I saw the displaced rail. I heard no pounding of any kind coming from under the car Union Square. The only pounding I recall is that which I heard when someone who climbed up on the roof of the car which was on the bridge. I watched the man lean over and use a sledge in knocking out the window of the car."

But the plaintiffs argued that because the train was behind schedule and the streamliner was trying to make up for lost time, the speed was too much for a weak spot in curve 613. The tremendous strain forced it to give way. Also, the investigations by railroad police, FBI, ICC, and Nevada state authorities produced no one connected with the purported crime. And, furthermore, there were discrepancies in the evidence, particularly with regard to the use of a buda-jack in moving the receiving rail. Finally, the Wallors argued that it should be borne in mind that most of the defendant's witnesses were employees of the defendant railroad company.

Their response was that

"We admit defendants have made a satisfactory explanation of the cause of the wreck, but nevertheless they were still negligent. We claim that the block signals were inadequate because the bond wires uniting the rails and forming a part of the signal system were too long, permitting the rails to be moved without severing connection. Such condition could have been avoided by using shorter wires or a rigid connection between rails."

But Southern Pacific lawyers countered that the signal system installed and operated was in accordance with law and approved railroad practice. Ordinary track laborers can easily become familiar with railroad signal systems and their operation. They would have no difficulty in making a workable connection whether the bond wires were short or long, or whether there was a rigid connection between the rails. The operation is a simple one and any evil-minded person can misaline a track.

The plaintiffs then concluded by accusing Southern Pacific of violating a 1913 Nevada statute which said that a locomotive must be equipped with a headlight of at least fifteen hundred candlepower. SP responded that the state law did not apply in this case since Congress had occupied the field and that a state law must yield to a federal law.

Upon a careful consideration of the case, Judge St. Sure rendered the opinion that the plaintiffs had failed to sustain the burden of proof by the preponderance of evidence. He had to conclude that the plaintiffs "take nothing by their action against the defendants and that the defendants have judgment for their costs."

★　★　★

Even though the Wallors' evidence was entirely circumstantial, their arguments were both interesting and sticky. For example, they pointed out that,

*Even if Southern Pacific had made a satisfactory explanation, it was still negligent. There had been a "violation" of the signal inspection act (49 U.S.C.A. 26).

*Southern Pacific admitted the train was overrunning its headlights; bond wires were used on the misalined track which would permit a rail to be moved 19 inches without triggering the signal to stop.

*Southern Pacific had the responsibility to have signals which would show the position of track (So. Ry Co. V. Hussey, 283 U.S. 136 and Sinan V. Santa Fe, 103 C.A. 703 284 Pac. 1041). The signal system gave a false indication of the condition of the track, even if Southern Pacific admitted tampering with the rail. This could have been avoided by a shorter bond wire or a rigid connection between rails.

*Southern Pacific violated the Nevada Complied Laws of 6332 which required that lights show a man at 1000 feet and make no exception for curves.

*Limited vision contributed to the derailment since Hecox saw an object 300 feet away and knew he could not slow down materially in the short distance.

*Hecox was trying to make up time. Overturning speed was 120 miles per hour. There was no proof the track could stand up under such speed. Also, no one knows for sure how fast the train was going except Hecox.

*The train derailed after the sixth unit, which then pulled the head end off. The Wallors argued, "It is hard to believe the head end could slide across the bridge. Southern Pacific states that the guard rail upset this theory. If the power unit slid 900 feet, more damage would have resulted to the sides of the power units. There was none. Only the ties caught fire near the west side. Why did not the oil in the gear cases catch fire?"

*The vandals have not been found. Strangers would have been noticed in the sparsely settled country. Also, the tools were too heavy to be carried to the derailment site.

*The act of sabotage was supposed to have occurred between 6:30 p.m. and sundown, around 6:42 p.m. There was not enough time to move a rail over nearly 5 inches in distance.

*The quick-drying enamel was not dry. There was opportunity to plant this piece of evidence, including the paint brush and enamel lid.

*Tie no. 1 west was badly split and a spike could have been driven without much effort.

*If a person were planning the derailment in advance, he would have used black paint. There would be no reason in painting the rail black. The tumble weed was sufficient to hide

the open joint. The use of paint was just an effort on Southern Pacific's part to make the job look perfect.

*There were no wheel marks on tie no. 1 west.

*There were no wheel marks on the base of the receiving rail.

*It would not be unusual to find lost tools in the river.

*No one would have carefully planned this derailment before hand and then thrown evidence all over the place afterwards.

*It was entirely possible that some volunteer in doing rescue work in the warm climate took off his jacket and threw it in the river.

*The jack had nothing to do with the accident. The FBI proved that it was from the tool box of the bridge crew.

*Southern Pacific offered no pictures of the ties near the north rail east of the bridge or of the ties on the bridge. The cars could not have run over the bridge on the ties because of the very small side clearance and guard rails.

*In September of 1939, Southern Pacific had reduced speed over similar curves. A speed of 60 miles an hour was considered dangerous.

*If there had been an open bridge, the casualties would have been fewer.

*And, most crucial of all, the entire batch of witnesses were the defendant's employees.

Needless to say, the attorneys for the plaintiffs were bitter over St. Sure's decision. They felt they had clearly demonstrated how the engineer must depend upon signals. Yet, the signals did not reveal the condition of the track ahead of the train on the night of August 12. Even if the rail had been painted, the engineer should have seen that one whole rail was out.

Also, it was impossible to accept that the pilot of the power unit scraped paint off the rail and then slid 900 feet still leaving paint on the pilot. The paint could have been placed there afterwards.

Further, it was odd that only the lid of the paint can, plus a small paint brush were found. The draft from the passing streamliner would have blown the lid away. And, if the tumble weed had been there, it should have received some damage.

In short, the attorneys argued that evidence of a carefully planned derailment could not reconcile the carelessness afterwards. A person bent on derailing the City of San Francisco would have learned something about its construction. A better site would have been picked.

The attorneys went so far as to suggest that track foreman Bianchini who lived in Harney could have planted evidence before Fogus and Hecox arrived under the car. In their thinking, the investigation was made from a biased point of view in hopes of finding evidence to support the sabotage theory. They should have won the case, they told reporters, because it is the responsibility of the railroad to guard every inch of its track. Obviously, Southern Pacific hadn't done so.

★   ★   ★

With the outbreak of the war on December 7th, 1941, O'Connell's leads dwindled. During the previous Fall, only 23 new tips came in, the lowest number for a similar period of time since the derailment. This may have been due to people who formerly would have taken an interest in helping Southern Pacific were now concentrating on helping law enforcement agencies fight the possible sabotage of the war effort.

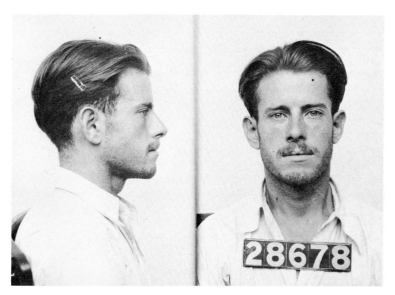

Roy O'Hara

Robert O'Hara

After Pearl Harbor, O'Connell and his men were assigned the responsibility of protecting government property and war shipments.

However, two leads were worthy enough to have several agents investigate them. One dealt with information received from an ex-convict concerning two other ex-convicts, Robert and Roy O'Hara, twin brothers who were on parole from San Quentin at the time of the derailment. According to the information, the O'Hara brothers were working on a poultry farm near Reno when the train was sabotaged. Agents verified that the two men did not work on the afternoon of August 12. They had evidently left the farm in their automobile and did not return until the following morning.

On January 8th, 1940, the two violated their parole by getting drunk and disturbing the peace. They were quickly returned to prison. While in prison they were quoted as saying they derailed the streamliner for the purpose of looting the dead passengers. But their plans miscarried when the wreck was not as great as they had anticipated. They also were quoted as saying the investigation was too hot and that the safest place for them was back in prison. Therefore, they violated their parole.

The O'Hara brothers were released in August of 1940. Roy moved to Berkeley, California, and became a chief suspect since he was reputed to be the type of criminal who was so daring he would commit any crime if there was enough money in it.

Roy was immediately arrested and questioned by Berkeley police and Southern Pacific agents as to his whereabouts in August of 1939. He admitted that he and his brother had worked on that poultry farm near Reno during that month. Although O'Connell established that Roy was not working on the afternoon of August 12th, O'Hara was evasive and claimed that he and his brother went to

Reno for a night on the town. He argued that they were in a night club when word was received of the tragedy. He also insisted they never visited the scene of the wreck.

O'Hara then confided who he thought informed on him and why the man had a grudge. It seems Roy developed an interest in the man's wife. The man was jealous and wanted to punish him for good. O'Hara claimed that his return to San Quentin for parole violation was not a deliberate result to avoid questioning as the informant believed. On the contrary, Roy insisted his arrest for parole violation resulted from the wife's husband having friends in the police department.

Though O'Connell's men made a careful investigation of the brothers, they were unable to develop any tangible evidence that either participated in the crime.

★　★　★

The Chief Special Agent then turned his attention to the possibility that the unusual stitches sewn on the tan jacket might have been done by someone who formerly lived in Coffee County, Tennessee, where most of America's baseballs were made.

Samples of baseball thread were obtained, as well as samples of the types of sewing, single and double stitch, used in covering the exterior of the balls. Comparing those with the sewing on the tan jacket demonstrated a definite similarity. Both were known as "single stitch." There was also a good deal of similarity between one type of thread used in sewing baseballs and the thread with which the jacket was made.

However, the thread with which the jacket was sewed proved to be a three-ply thread. O'Connell learned that three-ply thread was not used by the

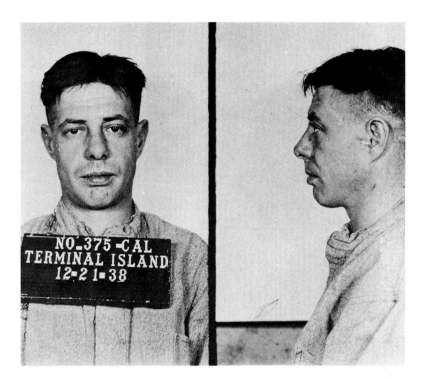

James Thompson

baseball manufacturers of Coffee County, but that it was a major manufacturing technique used in Mexico. Furnished with the names of Mexican firms who make thread for baseball sewing purposes, O'Connell sent a number of his agents to Mexico City to investigate. However, nothing materialized from such an investigation.

Meanwhile, further investigation was made in Tennessee to determine if any former resident of Coffee County had a grudge against Southern Pacific.

★ ★ ★

Among the tips investigated during the early part of 1942 concerned A. Coffey of Seattle, Washington. This man telephoned the Southern Pacific ticket office in Seattle on August 15th, 1939, asking if a reward had been offered in the derailment case. He explained he could not identify himself, other than to give his name as A. Coffey. The next day, he wrote a letter addressed to "Special Agent, SP Comp., Ogden," in which he insisted he knew the names of the train wreckers. Southern Pacific was to acknowledge his letter with an advertise-

Leonard Rosenberg

161

ment in the Seattle want ads. This was done. On September 18th, another letter was received in Ogden naming the ringleaders as James P. Thompson, 208 Main Street, Seattle, and M. Rosenberg, 1338 Pacific Ave., Tacoma, Washington.

This data was immediately turned over to the FBI. But little progress had been made when they withdrew their active participation in the case.

In December of 1942, Alex Coturri, a special agent assigned to the SP office in Portland, finally tracked down Thompson. Coturri discovered that Thompson was a lecturer for the "I Won't Work" Socialist group. It seems that on the night of August 12th, he had given a lecture for the I.W.W. in Spokane. Later that evening, he boarded a train for Chicago in order to continue his lecture tour. Thompson insisted he did not know anyone by the name of Rosenberg or Coffey. As far as he knew, these men were not members of the I.W.W.

Coturri was unable to locate Rosenberg. However, a few months later, the agent received a letter from an ex-convict named Leonard Rosenberg indicating that Captain Osborne of the Tacoma police department had informed him that Coturri wanted to see him.

The agent immediately left for Tacoma in order to question him. A check of Rosenberg's story revealed that he was in Seattle on August 12th, 1939, and this eliminated him from further suspicion. This false lead had been the longest under investigation by either the FBI or Southern Pacific agents.

★　★　★

In early January of 1943, a United Press item appeared in the San Francisco "EXAMINER" indicating an attempt had been made to tamper with tracks on the Pennsylvania Railroad near Stanton, Delaware, an hour before a special train carrying President Roosevelt passed by. Chief Special Agent Alan Bonner sent O'Connell a report which indicated the tampering was similar to the manner in which the track at Harney had been misalined. However, an intensive investigation proved futile.

★　★　★

Late that summer, J. Edgar Hoover wired O'Connell that Frank Elwell Irwin, a tent and cable repairman for the Hennies Brothers traveling carnival performing in Huntington, West Virginia, recognized the tan jacket on a circular posted in the main post office as one he stitched for an unknown man in July of 1939. Irwin told an FBI agent that the Hennies Brothers show was traveling in the western states and had played the week of July 4th in Boise. On successive weeks during 1939, the carnival was in Yakima and Spokane. In order to facilitate setting up the show in Spokane on Monday evening, July 24th, 1939, a number of local men were hired. At about 5:30 p.m., a man approached him and asked if he would repair some rips he had just received in his jacket. Irwin said that he did not know the man. Evidently, the fellow came to him because he sewed the carnival's torn canvas. The jacket was torn in two places, one on the left shoulder and the other on the top edge of the right pocket which opened at an angle near the waist. Irwin described the tear on the shoulder as two or three inches long and straight up and down. The jacket was made of an artificial rubberized suede cloth with a nap surface and unlined in buckskin color. The nap had been worked off in places leaving a slick surface. During the conver-

Frank Irwin, alias Sam Alexander

sation with the man, Irwin suggested trading jackets. But when Irwin tried on the stranger's jacket and found it a size too small, he decided to drop the idea. Irwin explained that he wore a size 40 which would have made this jacket size 38.

Irwin could not recall the type of stitch or thread used, although he furnished the agent with three sample thread types he generally used. He explained he probably used the simplest which he called "ball underhand." During the few minutes it took to repair the jacket, Irwin said he did not pay particular attention to the man, nor could he recall what they talked about. When the job was finished, the man thanked him and said he was about to leave for Coeur d'Alene, Idaho, and later for Wells, Nevada. The man was obviously a floater, many of whom came to the carnival for a day's work in setting up or taking down equipment. Irwin was certain the man was traveling as a hobo on freight trains. He hadn't asked why the fellow was going to Wells, nor did he think he could ever recognize him again.

★ ★ ★

The officer assigned to the Carlin area concluded his visits to the various section gangs between Ryndon and Winnemucca. During the years that followed the derailment, he showed the original jackets to 59 section foremen and laborers, as well as to the 12 members of steel gang no. 1002. The jackets were also displayed to 32 other employees and nine sheriffs and deputies in the vicinity. During these checks, not one of them could recognize the jackets as having been owned by anyone he knew, nor could he furnish any information to assist the investigation.

During this time, however, the agent received a tip from a resident in Carlin that certain members of gang no. 1002 were Communists and had made derogatory remarks about democracy and President Roosevelt. In view of the proximity of the steel gang to the scene of the derailment, each member was questioned and investigated at length.

The agent discovered that in arguments between various members of the gang over world conditions, two members had undoubtedly made a number of radical remarks. They also expressed disagreement with various policies of the Roosevelt administration. However, both men stoutly denied being members of the communist party or the German-American Bund. Indeed, they were opposed to both communist and fascist doctrines. Each insisted his remarks had been made during the height of heated discussions with fellow members of their steel gang and had to be considered in that light. It appeared that while both men were of a somewhat radical nature, there was

Jerry Craven

no concrete evidence to connect either with membership in foreign parties.

O'Connell instructed the agent to call upon the FBI office in Salt Lake City to inquire whether its undercover agents had picked up any tips that communists or fascists were responsible for the derailment. After checking the FBI files, O'Connell was advised they did not contain any information that would implicate such groups.

★ ★ ★

In the summer of 1943, O'Connell devoted a great deal of time to clue no. 163. This one above all the others preoccupied his thoughts although he had no substantial evidence upon which to base his feelings. The clue dealt with Jerry Craven, a former watchman at the Palisade Canyon Quarry.

It seems that at one time, Craven was a section foreman in the Salt Lake division. However, for various reasons, he had been demoted. When he was working as quarry watchman at Palisade in 1938, and again in 1939, a general tire inspector for Southern Pacific reported that he was most careless and untidy in his housekeeping. Since this could lead to a fire in the quarry, Tom Attix recommended that Craven's position be discontinued.

Within Southern Pacific, it was common knowledge that Craven was erratic, troublesome, and emotionally unstable. Some of his trouble stemmed from marital difficulties, since Mrs. Craven was known to be "consorting" with other men. She and their children lived in the old stationbuilding in Palisade while Craven stayed in a shack boardering a new irrigation unit near the quarry. However, he made frequent trips from the quarry to Palisade to see his wife and visit the children.

Jerry Craven's shack near the quarry where he served as
night watchman.

After the derailment, Craven was interviewed
on a number of occasions by both FBI and SP
agents. Each time that he was interviewed, he
maintained that he was in his shack near the
quarry on the night of August 12th. After dinner
around 6:00 p.m., he listened to his favorite radio
programs until 11:00 p.m., then crawled in bed. He
claimed he knew nothing of the wreck until the
next morning when Jim Eustler, a trackwalker,
told him about it. Craven said that he then drove to
Palisade to pick up his wife and children for a ride
out to the scene.

But the suspicion of the agents was aroused.
Quiet observations were made of Craven's movements. He was contacted by various operatives
under different pretexts in order for the conversations to lead up to the derailment. Hopefully, the
man might contradict himself somewhere along
the line. But Craven always repeated the same

story as to what he did on that fateful night.
Though O'Connell learned that Craven had on
some occasion left the quarry without having
Southern Pacific authorization to do so, not one
shred of evidence turned up disproving that he was
alone in his shack listening to his radio.

When his position as quarry watchman was
abolished in late August of 1940, Craven worked
for a short time as a trackwalker on the Palisade
section. During this time, his wife divorced him.
She and the children moved to Ogden. There, she
married Ray Hawkins, a former resident of
Palisade.

In October, Craven was transferred to the position of pumper in Wendel, Nevada. While working
at this during the next few years, various pretexts
were created so that agents could continue to interview him. On each occasion, Craven expressed
the hope that the saboteurs would be captured.

Dan O'Connell as a railroad detective in 1910.

Invariably, he would mention that if he had any information he would surely pass it on in hopes of obtaining the $10,000 reward.

In August of 1943, O'Connell arranged for an undercover agent to work along side of him. Hopefully, the man would gain Craven's confidence. Perhaps something would slip, or a contradiction made during a drunken stupor, or argument. Although the operative became very close to Craven, he was unsuccessful in obtaining any information which might implicate the man.

★ ★ ★

In July of 1944, the FBI formally withdrew from further investigation in the case since it occurred prior to the passage of the federal train wrecking law which had given F.B.I investigative jurisdiction. Actually, the FBI had withdrawn its agents years before, but now the bureau made it formal. With its active participation ending in early 1940, it passed on to O'Connell all its unfinished work, including reports covering the investigations it performed.

★ ★ ★

After relentlessly searching for the saboteurs day and night for five long years, Chief Special Agent Dan O'Connell retired in December of 1944. Known to thousands of friends as Dan, O'Connell cleaned his desk and left Southern Pacific. Although he was proud to have followed every single lead to its conclusion, he was deeply disappointed that the biggest case of his career had not been broken. He was succeeded by Andrew J. McKenna, his chief assistant.

A tall, courageous Irishman, O'Connell became a legend on the trail of criminals. Backed by his persuasive arguments, he could make even the toughest suspects talk.

In his colorful career, he came up against the murderous DeAutremont brothers, slippery Roy Gardner, and other infamous criminals. As the head of the largest private police force in America, he was feared as a deadly enemy. By the time he laid down his badge, O'Connell had made the profession of train robbery so hazardous that no Southern Pacific train had been successfully robbed since 1933.

Although primarily devoted to the prevention and detection of crime, he was equally proud of the fact that he helped protect all the presidents of the United States since Theodore Roosevelt, riding with them while they traveled the Southern Pacific line.

O'Connell's work had not always been spectacular. His army of special agents, at one point reaching 700, had the routine task of protecting more than 8,000 miles of railroad track extending from Oregon to New Mexico and Utah.

Born in Ireland, O'Connell arrived in the United States when he was 19. He had already attained the erect, muscular figure that was to stay with him the rest of his life. Soon, he found his way to California where he chose to work as a section man for Southern Pacific near Merced. Before long he was foreman.

One day a train struck a small obstruction that had been placed on the track by a few little girls. Although no damage was done, O'Connell turned in such an intelligent report that Chief Special Agent Patrick Kindelon invited the young man to drop in and see him the next time he was in San Francisco. When O'Connell eventually did, he found a job on the railroad police force waiting for him. He became a special agent shortly after the fire and earthquake of 1906.

Now, as his 70th birthday approached, and with it an inescapable retirement, O'Connell bought a home in San Francisco so that his two sons, Daniel, Jr., 15, and Kevin, 9, could be near the school of their choice. Together with his wife Helen, a registered nurse who cared for him 18 years previously when he was a patient in the Southern Pacific hospital, he polished the last chapters of a book he was writing dealing with his career. Yet, his bitterest disappointment after 43 years of service was that the saboteurs were still loose somewhere in America.

A summary of all the suspects he investigated is as follows:

Persons interviewed by O'Connell	12,579
Trespassers removed from trains and SP property and questioned by railroad detectives; their reports read by O'Connell	197,858
Total number of persons interviewed and reports studied by O'Connell up to his retirement	210,437

The power car of the City of San Francisco.

CONCLUSION

For a brief moment of time, the tragedy of the City of San Francisco stirred the sympathy of the American people. Everywhere, everyone hoped the saboteurs would be caught. But with the passage of the years, the dramatic event grew dim. By 1950, even the mere trickle of letters and "tips" ceased to come in.

And, the sad fact remained that in spite of all the imagination and endurance shown by railroad detectives in their followup of 1,144 major leads, no one was indicted.

Because of the dearth of new information, only one special agent remained on the case after the spring of 1950. Dan Murphy was permanently stationed in Carlin to seek out and become friends with those residents still living in the vicinity. Over the following seven years, Murphy gained widespread friendship with railroad employees and other Carlin, Beowawe, and Palisade residents.

At the time of the derailment, O'Connell realized that many people in the area were reluctant to divulge their suspicions since they were often working side by side with suspects, their families, and neighbors. It was thought that with the many changes in the communities over the 10 to 15 year period, conversations about the derailment might reawaken someone's interest in the case. Some obscure resident might mention an undisclosed, uninvestigated piece of information.

Murphy reinterviewed hundreds of residents. To his discouragement, he discovered that a number of old timers had since passed away. During the years of his work, not one new lead developed. In fact, most of those interviewed said it was the first mention of the case in years.

While these interviews did not unearth a new lead, they served to refreshen the recollection of the people questioned. It was Murphy's hope that if anyone remembered anything new he would bring it directly to him since all the nearby communities knew he was still working on the case.

Today, all the physical evidence of the derailment is still carefully protected in the room especially designed for it in the basement of the Southern Pacific building in San Francisco. Within a moment's notice, a new lead can be compared or matched to all that has ever been known in the case. One of the two keys required to enter the evidence room is still in the possession of the chief special agent. The other key is held by accounting department officials.

Thus ends the story of the most malicious tampering in railroad history. Although the Southern Pacific Company is prepared to pay the original $10,000 reward for information leading to an arrest and conviction, it can be confided that among retired as well as current railroad detectives one man stands out above all the others as the chief suspect. For nearly 40 years, officials knew "intuitively" that one of their own employees was the guilty party and that he probably acted alone. O'Connell, as well as all the other chief special agents who followed, investigated and reinvestigated the man. But, as much as their intuitive processes sensed that he was the mass killer, they could not come up with one single scrap of evidence for an arrest. That fellow is now dead and it may be that he carried the final answer to his grave.

On a happier note, Tony Firpo eventually married Cristina. After a long engagement spanning half the continent, the two were married in the summer of 1941. After serving as a lieutenant in the U.S. army during the crusade for Europe, Toe, as he was affectionately called by his wife and friends, returned to Stockton, California, to work for the U.S. post office service. Today, he and his wife are retired, helping to raise some 12 grandchildren.

As far as Thelma Ristvedt is concerned, the young stewardess who so courageously saved countless lives, promptly returned to work aboard the streamliner, Treasure Island Special, which replaced the City of San Francisco. In defiance to possible further acts of sabotage, she along with 172 passengers boarded the very first eastbound train within a week of the tragedy.

Although deluxe accommodations and service were provided, and although the substitute streamliner closely resembled her predecessor in appearance and color schemes, she was not, and never could be, the City of San Francisco.

APPENDICES
FOLLOWING

Appendix One

MEMORANDUM OF INFORMATION AND INSTRUCTIONS PERTAINING
TO OPERATION OF STREAMLINER "CITY OF SAN FRANCISCO".

This memorandum is prepared in this form to enable
employes to afford proper replies to passengers' questions
and to form a basis of uniform and proper method of procedure under routine and unusual circumstances.

1. General description of train:

Consists:

```
         2 power unit cars
         2 head end cars
         1 diner-lounge
         3 standard sleeping cars
         1 Pullman room car
         1 coach
         1 coach-buffet
        ── ──────────────
        11 cars (Total)
```

       Total weight of train - 530 tons.

       Total length of train - 725 feet.

The two power unit cars cannot be separated from each
other except when in the shop but the two together can be
uncoupled from the baggage car. None of the other nine cars
can be separated on the road.

The power units consist of two 1200 h.p. 2 cycle 16
cylinder V-type Diesel engines built by the Winton Engine
Corporation at Cleveland and installed by the Electro-
Motive Corporation in its plant near Chicago. One of
these engines is located in each power car. They are run
at a top speed of 750 revolutions per minute. They operate two electric generators which supply direct current
at maximum of 750 volts to eight traction motors, one of
which is geared to each of the eight axles under the two
power cars. The drive wheels are 36 1/8 inches in diameter.
All other wheels are 34 inches.

2. Speed:

The average speed between Chicago and Oakland Pier is

56½ m.p.h. The average speed Ogden to Oakland Pier is 52
m.p.h., and Ogden to Sparks is 62½ m.p.h. The maximum
speed attained on trial trips was 115 m.p.h. The maximum allowed in regular service is 95 m.p.h. Time between
Chicago and San Francisco - 39 3/4 hours.

3. Passenger capacity:

            84 beds in sleeping cars
            86 seats in coaches

4. Schedule:

Train is scheduled to leave San Francisco 3:40 p.m.
and Oakland Pier at 4:10 p.m. on the 2nd, 8th, 14th, 20th
and 26th of each month. Arrives Chicago at 9:30 a.m. C.S.T.
on the 4th, 10th, 16th, 22nd and 28th of each month.
Leaves Chicago at 6:15 p.m. on the 5th, 11th, 17th, 23rd
and 29th and arrives San Francisco at 7:52 a.m. on the 7th,
13th, 19th, 25th, and 31st (or 1st) of each month.

5. Dining service:

The highest type of dining car service is provided in
the diner-lounge car. Cooks and waiters are on duty all
night. Equally good food at much less cost is provided in
the coaches and served from the buffet at extreme rear of
train. Three meals may be had in coaches for a total cost
of $1.10.

Pillows are provided coach passengers without charge.
At night color lights are used in coaches to provide a
restful effect for comfort of passengers.

The waiters in coaches also serve as attendants.

Features of Operation

1. Starting:

Inasmuch as the engineer is seated near the middle
of the cab he cannot see hand signals given by trainmen

alongside the train, hence the signal to start should always be given by conductor using the air signal button, one of which is located over the doorway of each coach exit as well as in baggage cars.

The proper procedure at the regular stops is to open one Pullman car trap and the trap at head end of rear coach. The train will be stopped at exactly the same spot each trip. Station force is expected to have the Pullman and coach passengers who are to entrain directed to the proper spot on platform so they may promptly board the train in sleeping cars or coaches as the case may be. No visitors should board the train as stops en route are too brief to permit of doing so. One minute before due to depart or as soon as passengers are loaded, the rear brakeman should board the head end of rear coach, close the trap and door, open small window in door and signal conductor that rear of train is ready. Conductor and head brakeman should likewise board the Pullman car, close the trap and door before leaving time and, after receiving hand signal from rear brakeman as above referred to, conductor will, when leaving time arrives, signal engineer with two blasts of the air signal. Engineer will proceed at once unless train is covered by blue flag. In case of any delay in moving, rear brakeman should proceed to telephone in kitchen end of rear coach and have an understanding with the engineer as to cause and probable length of delay and if necessary to go out flagging, advise engineer to that effect. When coach door and trap are open an attendant must remain on duty to guard it and request passengers to remain on the train.

This procedure must be understood by all and strictly adhered to, otherwise complications, delays and possibly personal injuries may result.

2. Procedure at regular stopping points:

Eastward:

Passenger stops are made at -

    16th Street, Oakland
    Berkeley, University Avenue
    Sacramento
    Reno
    Ogden

At 16th Street and Berkeley one trap will be opened in each sleeping car and each coach to expedite entraining passengers. Employes will request visitors not to board train. As soon as passengers are on all employes will board train, close traps and doors and be prepared to start train on time as above instructed.

At Sacramento and Reno, Pullman employes will open traps between cars 27 and 28 and coach attendant will open trap at head end of rear coach. Train will stop at same spot each trip. Station force will direct Pullman and coach passengers to the proper locations on platform where traps referred to will to will be opened.

At Sacramento and Reno hand baggage of Pullman passengers will be loaded in vestibule of car 28 and Pullman passengers through vestibule of car 27.

Passengers should be loaded and unloaded promptly, employes board cars, close traps and be prepared to start train on time in manner as above instructed.

Bear in mind conductor alone is authorized to give starting signal and that he must use the air signal for that purpose. Engine-men are instructed not to accept hand signals for starting.

Operating stops, eastward, as follows:

Roseville to change engine crews. Rear brakeman will station himself at service door on right side of train and unless some unusual delay ensues will not have time to leave the train. Conductor will signal engineer with air signal to proceed as soon as engineer sounds engine bell or whistle indicating ready. Conductor should remain on train unless some unusual delay develops in which event he should telephone engineer to ascertain cause and have an understanding as to flagging. Incoming engineer will transfer train orders to outgoing engineer.

Colfax - Stop to pick up steam engine for helper to Norden. Head brakeman will promptly detrain from baggage car and handle switches for helper. As soon as coupled to train he and conductor will board train and latter will give proceed air signal in usual way. Engineer of Streamliner will pass proceed signal to steam engineer. When stop made at Colfax the rear brakeman will leave the train from service door on right side of kitchen at rear of train. Coach stops and door will not be opened.

NORDEN. Procedure same as at Colfax. Train crew will work from baggage car door at head end and kitchen service door at rear.

Sparks. Conductors and head brakemen will change through baggage car door. Rear brakemen will change through kitchen service door on right side rear end of rear coach. No Pullman or coach traps or doors will be opened as it is very undersirable for passengers to detrain at Sparks and they should be informed that passengers may leave train at Ogden only. Just prior to leav-

ing time, trainmen should be aboard and rear brakeman should indicate to conductor by lantern signal that he is aboard, and at leaving time conductor should give air signal to start. If train does not promptly move he should telephone engineer and be governed according to understanding with him.

Ice will be supplied through doors on right side of train without lowering steps or necessity of Pullman or coach attendants to leave train.

Carlin. No Pullman or coach traps will be opened. Head brakemen and conductors will change through baggage car door. Rear brakeman through kitchen service door on right side rear coach. In coming rear brakeman will protect rear of train until departs. Outgoing rear brakeman will be provided with flagging equipment to hand to incoming man who will protect train while standing at Carlin. Outgoing rear brakeman will as soon as train stops board it through kitchen service door on right side of rear coach, close door and indicate to conductor with lantern signal that he is aboard. At leaving time conductor will give air signal to depart and if train does not move on time will telephone engineer for information as to delay.

Ogden. Train will use track No. 1. All Pullman and coach traps on left side will be opened to permit passengers to detrain if they so desire. Departure of train will be announced in waiting room and dining room of station.

Westward: Regular passenger stops:
Reno
Sacramento
Berkeley
16th Street, Oakland

Traps will be opened only on cars where passengers are to enter or leave train. Trainmen will be governed as above instructed in that they will board train, close steps and doors and be prepared to depart on time or without any delay.

Operating stops: Carlin
Sparks
Roseville

Trainmen at Carlin and Sparks will change through baggage car at head end and through service door in kitchen on right side of rear coach. No coach traps or doors will be opened. Outgoing rear man will be provided with flagging equipment to hand to incoming brakeman who will protect train while standing at Carlin.

Engine crews will change at Roseville. Engineers will change via cab ladder. Firemen through head baggage car door. No coach or Pullman traps will be opened at Roseville. If any delay, rear brakeman and conductor will confer with engineer by telephone and be governed by verbal understanding.

Unusual stops en route at any time

Rear brakeman will promptly telephone engineer for information and instructions as to probable delay and have an understanding as to flagging. Conductor will also phone engineer.

Telephones are located in kitchen of rear coach and in the two head end cars behind power units. To talk or listen, press button on the combination receiver-transmitter. There is a loud speaker in the cab. The engineer has a transmitter through which he can answer a trainman but he has no means of calling a trainman to a phone.

8

Hand brakes:

There are three hand brakes - one in each motor unit and one in the kitchen end of rear car.

If the power unit or air brakes fail, the train should be secured with these hand brakes. Likewise if it becomes necessary to uncouple motor units from other cars, the hand brakes in head and rear cars must be set before motor unit is uncoupled. These brakes are very effective and must be released before train is moved, otherwise wheels will be slid flat.

Air Brakes:

There are no retainer valves on this train. Running air brake tests should be made at same point each trip and brakes applied sufficiently to insure rear brakeman being able to determine when done. He will signal engineer with air signal 16 (h) - five short blasts.

Straight air braking system is used, hence no rear end air test is made when train is being handled by the Diesel power units. In event of motor failure and steam engine is coupled ahead or if double-headed with steam engine, the automatic braking system is used and same rules apply as with steam service, except there are no retainer valves to operate.

Backup movements:

It may occasionally happen that short backup movements will have to be made, also long backup movements by reason of main track being blocked. Following will govern when such movements have to be made.

Conductor and one of his brakemen will station themselves in the kitchen end of the rear coach. Conductor will take up a position on the right side of train (looking toward the head end) and by means of the telephone inform the engineer when he is ready to make the backup movement and at the same time test the air signal line by giving signal 16 (c) - three short blasts, and will then sound the siren located under the rear end of the train and which is operated by slowly opening the valve with the horizontal lever in the box below where the telephone is located where the conductor will be stationed as above instructed. The brakeman should station himself on the opposite side of the kitchen end and open the side window of the car over the serving table and through which he can lean out far enough to obtain view to the rear of the train. With the conductor and one brakeman so located they can command a view to the rear under normal conditions and conductor by means of the telephone should indicate to engineer the speed which he considers safe to use and frequently converse with the engineer to make sure the telephone is in operative condition and engineer is able to hear what instructions the conductor has to give. It is should happen the telephone should fail or engineer does not promptly respond to the conductor's instructions, the latter should then immediately resort to the use of the air signal located immediately above the telephone, and if an extreme emergency arises requiring an immediate stop the conductor should use the valve which is in a vertical position in the box below the telephone, but the brakes should not be thus applied from the rear except to avoid an accident as there is danger of sliding the wheels when using the emergency at low speed. The telephone cord is long enough to reach to the opposite

side of the car in the event the conductor finds it necessary to cross to the opposite side to see what is going on and at the same time be able to use the telephone. The equipment at hand is ample to insure safety in making back-up movement under ordinary conditions, but in the event of darkness or stormy weather it may be necessary in the judgment of the conductor to afford flag protection ahead of the train while making backup movement.

Emergencies: In case of derailment or necessity for immediate stop, trainmen will use conductor's emergency valve. A short red cord is located in hallway at end of each car. The use of cord should be restricted to extreme emergencies. Quick results can always be obtained by using the air signal and if time permits use the telephone.

General Service: If passengers request any changes in temperature, lighting, etc., in coaches, trainmen will ask the attendant to do what is necessary. Trainmen will not handle lighting or other switches. Pullman and dining car employes will take care of such matters in sleeping cars and diner, but this does not relieve trainmen of seeing to it that cars are kept comfortable. If more steam heat pressure is necessary in cold weather, conductor will notify fireman or man on duty in motor room.

Conclusion: This train differs in various respects from equipment we have been accustomed to and represents the best that modern talent and engineering has produced. It is of utmost importance that crews be alert and be in their proper positions with car steps up, doors closed and ready to proceed on time. This is an excess fare train. Nothing should be left undone to cater to the comfort, convenience and safety of the passengers.

G. E. Gaylord   W. L. Hack   J.C. Goodfellow

Appendix Two

```
XXXXXXXXXXXXXXXXXXXXXXXXXXXXXXXXXXX
X                                 X
X      GENERAL INFORMATION AND    X
X    INSTRUCTIONS FOR ENGINEERS,  X
X   FIREMAN AND ALL CONCERNED     X
X   FOR HANDLING DIESEL ENGINES   X
X      -o-o-o-o-o-o-o-o-o-o-      X
X   THE NEW CITY OF SAN FRANCISCO X
X      -o-o-o-o-o-o-o-o-o-o-      X
X  AIR BRAKE QUESTIONS AND ANSWERS X
X        -o-o-o-o-o-o-o-o-        X
X          Charles A. Fogus       X
X  District Road Foreman of Engines X
X       Sacramento, California    X
X           July 1938             X
XXXXXXXXXXXXXXXXXXXXXXXXXXXXXXXXXXX
X              NOTICE             X
X   This pamplet is not of an     X
X   official nature and is present- X
X   ed to the engineers and others X
X   for instructions on Diesel-   X
X   Electric Power Units only.    X
X          PRICE 25 CENTS         X
X                                 X
XXXXXXXXXXXXXXXXXXXXXXXXXXXXXXXXXXX
```

INDEX

INSTRUCTIONS FOR ENGINEERS   -1-
HANDLING THE NEW CITY OF SAN FRANCISCO
-o-o-o-o-o-o-o-

Assuming that all engines are running and warmed up and that air pressure is up to standard, see for yourself that tanks are full of fuel and water by the indicating guage on right hand side and near the middle of each power unit. Before starting on the trip see that hand brakes are off, one on each of the three power units.
See that the isolation switches are down on all engines that are to be used.

Now to control room. Block brake valve handle down. Over the train control district - Oakland to Sparks see that key cut-out is at right angle to pipe in open position. Remove key and place in box provided for it. Also cut in safety control or Dead man valve is located on J application valve at right angle when open. Also see that engine cut-off devise is pulled out.

PROPER HANDLING OF THROTTLE

1. In starting train open throttle to run No. 1 momentarily, then run No. 2 and on up to No. 8. Be slow from No. 5 on up. Do not go to No. 8 until speed has reached 22 MPH.

After wheel slip light has flashed six times or a speed of 22 MPH is reached, open throttle to No. 8. the flash of the wheel slip light indicates transition of each power plant from series to parallel.

2. Transition from parallel to shunt and back to parallel will be automatic in operation without any change in throttle.

3. Should the wheel slip gauge show a white light continuously it indicates that a pair of traction wheels are slipping or sliding. Stop at once and locate cause.

HANDLING OF THROTTLE AND AIR BRAKES

1. When main throttle is being operated in position above run 5 and before brakes are applied to steady train on curves, the throttle must be closed to run 5 as indicated on throttle quadrant.

2. When speed of train is to be reduced to 18 MPH or less close the throttle to run one (1) before brakes are applied. If stop is to be made close throttle to idle position.

3. When drifting or before passing over railroad crossings throttle must be closed to run No. one (1) to avoid dropping contactors from parallel operation. Do not close throttle to idle position unless stop is to be made or speed is reduced to 18 MPH or less.

The traction motors develop the most drawbar pull - starting effort-when the engine is standing still. If one power unit stops and the throttle is not advanced it is very probably that all engines will stop.

          -2-

When opening the throttle to accelerate the train leave it in No. 1 (1) position just long enough for a little, or possibly all of the slack to be taken out of the couplers. Get throttle over to No. 2 (2) position as quickly as possible without jerking the train. Do not leave throttle in No. 1 (1) position as there is danger of stopping one or more engines.

In moving throttle from No. 2 (2) to No. 8 (8) position, open it from one position to the next only after the train has accelerated sufficiently to have relieved part of the load on the generator. Opening the throttle too quickly while the train is moving slowly puts an undue load on both mechanical and electrical equipment. Moreover if the throttle is opened too quickly there is the possibility that the governor will not have a chance to adjust itself to the load and the speed, with the result that the overspeed governor is very likely to cut in and stop the engines.

Should you stop one or more engines starting and no one is available to help you, stop. Apply brakes leaving brake valve handle in service. You can then leave the seat, go back to the stalled engine, raise the isolation switch, this will stop the alarm bell, if more than one engine stops do the same on the next engine. Start engine by pressing start button with right hand, as soon as engine starts release button and while idling see that lubricating oil pressure gauge shows 15 pounds. Close isolation switch, you may then release brakes and start.

CLOSING THE THROTTLE

When the throttle is to be closed or moved forward, do not move quickly from one position to the other. It takes a short interval of time for the governor control to readjust itself, during which time the heavy rotating and reciprocating parts of the power units must have a chance to slow up to the new condition.

Field observations point conclusively to the fact that quickly closing the throttle usually results in stuck exhaust valves. When the valves stick the fireman has trouble to say nothing of the possibility of the entire unit being effected sooner or later if this practice is continued. In the event of an emergency, it is permissible, of course, to quickly move the throttle all the way forward. In service stops, however, the throttle should always be moved slowly from one position to the other and a little time allowed before moving from one position to another.

HANDLING ON GRADES

Ascending grades when speed drops below 18 M.P.H. it will be necessary to drop back into series, do so by closing the throttle to idling position momentarily; this drops the parellel contactors out, then come out with throttle to No. 1 (1) position which picks up the series contactors.

Descending grades where power is not used for 30 minutes or over, pull out the field exciter switch, place horseshoe block back of it, run engines in No. 2 (2)

OPERATING BRAKES WHEN HELPER ENGINE IS TO BE ADDED ENROUTE

Make stop with straight air: hold brakes applied until the helper is coupled on—to prevent train from moving. Before air is cut through from helper, release straight air brakes. Next cut out Automatic train control get key from box to do so, then have air cut through from helper. Close double head cock in cab. Cut out Safety control or dead man valve handle at right angle to pipe and wire seal.

When helper engine is to be cut off after stop is made lap brake valve block handle down cut in double head cock. Cut in safety control or dead man valve to open position and seal. Then cut in Train Control valve remove key and place in box. Apply acknowledging valve to get white light in train control indicator. See that engine control button is pulled out then O K to release and start.

TO RELEASE AN AUTOMATIC TRAIN CONTROL APPLICATION

Place brake valve handle on lap, after stop is made hold brake valve handle down and wait for the red hand on the A.T.C., gauge to restore to normal pressure which will require 60 seconds, place handle of acknowledging valve in acknowledging position, or back, to restore white light in cab signal and then release brakes.

TO RELEASE AN EMERGENCY APPLICATION

Place brake valve on lap wait 15 seconds for vent valves to seat brake seal and move BA-4 cut out cock to extreme left hold foot pedal or brake valve handle down and release brakes, then return the BA-4 cut out cock to extreme right and re-seal, Pull out engine control button, if in Train control territory restore white light in indicator.

CUTTING OUT BRAKES

To cut out brakes on each power unit or car in train—as each is equipped with a D-22-C control valve—close the plug cock to this valve and bleed same by pressing release stem sideways.

To cut out brakes on any one truck on power units there are three cut out self - locking cocks. One cuts out the brakes to 4 brake cylinders on entire truck, next two will cut out 2 brake cylinders, leaving ½ of brakes working, all on one pair of traction wheels and ½ brakes on idler.

When necessary to handle train by automatic air brakes, after changing brake valve, you will have graduated release and there are ten blow-down type retaining valves. When this change is made on grades notify train crew so retainers may be used.

---

position to charge batteries and pump up air. Before stop is made close throttle to idling position. Before start is attempted remove horseshoe and push in field exciter button.

Use water on power unit wheels descending grades over 1% except Montello and Wells. To start water, first open the water valve handle located on the floor, right side by the second engine in each unit, then start the pump by the switch on the left side on the wall. Close the water valve when through and blow out the pipes with air to prevent freezing in cold weather.

CUTTING THE AUTOMATIC TRAIN CONTROL INTO SERVICE

In train control territory at terminals - Oakland - Sparks - electricians will cut in and out and test same.

A-1. Unlock three position selector switch and move switch handle to left - position marked S.P. - then replace hasp and lock.
2. Close main switch by pushing down on switch handle located at left of the voltage regulator.
3. Move handle of acknowledging switch to acknowledging position - white light will then be displayed indicating that A.T. C., electrical equipment is in operating condition.
4. Move handle of the key cut-out cock to right until it is at right angle to panel board located on "J".

Cutting the Automatic Train Control out of service.
1. Move the handle of key cut out cock to left until it is parallel to panel board or closed position. Then wire seal in closed position.
2. Cut out main switch.

WHEN HELPER ENGINES ARE ADDED ENROUTE

To open up front coupler, turn top and bottom latch ½ turn, pull the right door first as you face it, turn bottom latch to left door, pull out air hose and lift levers, then open left air valve, whistle will blow, lift up latch under coupler and pull cupler all the way out, close the left air valve, this will seat the pin and whistle will stop, all set to couple. While helper is attached leave air pressure on to hold pin down.

To replace the coupler, close right air valve, when air blows down open left air valve, whistle will blow indicating pin is up, then push coupler all the way in, then close left air valve, when air blows down open the right one, seating the pin and whistle will stop blowing, replace lifters, then air hose, left door, then right door and turn locks.

When helper engines are added enroute engineer of the Streamliner will handle the key cut-out cock of the A. T. C. - handle is parallel to the bracket when cut out, and at right angles when cut in.

STOPPING DISTANCES ON STRAIGHT AND LEVEL TRACK

M.P.H.	APPLICATION	DISTANCE	TIME
80	45 Lo. Bk Cyl.	3375 feet	57 Sec.
82	A.T.C.	4300 feet	57 Sec.
60	Slow service	2050 feet	42 Sec.
90	Slow service	3900 feet	57 Sec.

GENERAL INFORMATION

Length of Power Units. . . . . . . 209 Ft. 6 In.
Total weight of the three Power Units. . 878,360 lbs
Weight on drivers No. 1 Unit . . . . 202,580 lbs
Weight on drivers No. 2 Unit . . . . 196,772 lbs
Weight on drivers No. 3 Unit . . . . 196,440 lbs
Total weight on drivers three Units. . 595,792 lbs
Total weight of train. . . . . . 2,541,580 lbs
Total weight of train in "M's. . . . 2541 M's
Axle load No. 1 driver . . . . . 50,456 lbs
Axle load, the idler . . . . . . 48,586 lbs
Water capacity, each Unit. . . . . 1100 Gals
Fuel capacity, each Unit. . . . . 1200 Gals
Water consumption per hour, Steam Heat . 300 Gals
Water consumption per hour, Wheel Coolers 300 Gals
There are 30 trucks under the train, 72 pair of wheels, 12 places where train may be parted.
Wheel diameter, 36 inches on Power cars and train.
Longest rigid wheel base . . . . . 14 Ft. 1 In.
Length of longest car. . . . . . 84 Ft. 6 In.
Fuel consumption for tractive power plant - 3 Units . . . . 2 Gals. per mile.
Fuel consumption of Auxiliary Plant. .20 Gals. per Hr.
Auxiliary Fuel Capacity. . . . . .600 Gals.
Auxiliary engines, 600 H.P. each, 300 K.W., 220 Volts A.C.
Steam Heat Boiler evaporates 15 lbs water to 1 lb of fuel.
Maximum Speed of Engines . . . .750 R.P.M.
Maximum Voltage. . . . . . .750 D.C.
Maximum Amperage. 2000
Maximum Speed not to exceed. . . .116 M.P.H.
Maximum speed allowed. . . . . 95 M.P.H.

HAND BRAKES

One hand brake is provided in each Unit, being located along the left side at the rear of the No. 2 high voltage cabinet.

Each Power Unit has its own set of controls with a separate independent brake valve so each Unit may be handled independently.

Extreme care must be taken in the use of this brake to see that it is not left "ON" when the Unit (engine) is moved, as it connects to only one axle and set of wheels, the "DRAG" it produced might not be noticeable, particularly if all Power Units were running, and it is very probable that flat spots would be put on the wheels.

FIREMAN'S DUTIES

1. Check lubricating oil for proper level, should be 2 inches under "full" mark on bayonet oil gauge while engine is idling. Oil should be checked whenever possible while engines are idling at or to determine whether crank case oil level is losing or gaining.

2. See that all extra lubricating oil extra cans are full before leaving terminals.

3. See that fuel and water tanks are full by indicating gauge.

4. Carefully check and maintain engine water temperature on all engines while running or idling at or near 155 degrees; this includes the auxiliary engine for lights and heat.

5. Turn fuel and lubricating oil purolators on each engine every 30 minutes, also fuel filters on steam heat boilers which are in use.

6. Check level of water in engine cooling system expansion tank. Report to mechanic on duty any irregularities you may notice.

7. See instructions on operating of steam heat boilers, copy on wall by each boiler.

8. Descending grades over 1%, except between Montello and Wells, use water wheel coolers, when through with water blow the pipes out with air to prevent freezing in cold weather.

YARD AND HELPER ENGINE CREW HANDLING CITY OF SAN FRANCISCO

Give strict attention to fuel oil heaters to prevent fuel oil from being blown out of the measuring pipe. Keep the heaters shut off if consistent, use care in sanding, do all possible to prevent smearing this train.

Be careful of condensation thrown from stack.

SPEED ON CURVES

Speed is predicated on elevation and center of gravity which is 60.8 for the Diesel power as follows:

Degrees	Elevation	M.P.H.
1 Degree	3	90
2 "	4½	73
3 "	4½	60
4 "	6	55
5 "	5½	50
6 "	5½	45
8 "	4	35
10 "	4	32
10 "	No	10

SUPPLEMENT--CHANGE OF "DEADMAN" AND DECELAKRON OPERATION.

On the new CITY OF SAN FRANCISCO, changes have been made with the operation of the foot pedal, or "deadman" feature.

It has been changed so that when an application has been made intentionally or unintentionally, the stop will be made through the operation of the decelakron, which prevents an emergency stop.

When an application is received from either source, lap the brake valve, take the foot off the pedal for a moment, then hold (pedal down with brake valve on lap. It will require six (6) seconds for the red hand on control pipes to restore to normal pressure, which is 110 lbs. Brakes may then be released if it is not desired to stop.

If stop is desired remove foot from pedal, place the brake valve handle on lap, and train will be brought to a stop without jar or damage to wheels by decelakron control, which reduces the brake cylinder pressure as the speed of the train reduces.

To release, place foot on pedal, brake valve handle on lap, and wait for the red hand to restore to normal. Then, and not before, place brake valve handle in release.

This change nullifies the control of the Safety Control Cut-out Cock, and should be placed in No. 1 position and sealed.

The new cut-out cock is located on the "J" application valve, and should be sealed in open position. Cut out only when helper engine is attached.

A conductors valve has been attached to brake valve so that in case of failure of straight line same can be used to stop train.

AIR BRAKE QUESTIONS AND ANSWERS

17. Q. What is the purpose of the main reservoir check valve, and where is it located?

A. It is located at the entrance of the fourth main reservoir to prevent a back flow of air from brake system to the air operated devices; or in case of a broken pipe anywhere between the compressor and check valve.

20. Q. What pressure is contained in the fourth or last main reservoir?

A. Brake pipe pressure.

24. Q. Can the brake valve be changed to operate as an automatic brake valve?

A. Yes.

25. Q. How is this accomplished?

A. By a change over valve, operated by changing the handle of the brake valve from the operating portion to the change-over portion of the brake valve, which, when positioned, connects an equalizing piston and equalizing reservoir to the brake valve.

26. Q. Where is the equalizing piston located?

A. In the application valve of the automatic train control.

27. Q. Why is it located in this valve?

A. During an automatic train control application of the brakes, the equalizing piston functions in the same manner as with a manually initiated application, with the automatic brake valve.

28. Q. What are the functions of the brake valve?

A. Admits air to the automatic brake pipe, admits air to and exhausts it from the control reservoir, exhaust air from the safety control pipe to initiate a safety control application and provides a constant maximum adjustment on the decelakron when handle of brake valve is left in emergency position.

29. Q. Trace the flow of main reservoir air from the compressors to the various parts of the brake system.

A. From the compressors it flows to the surge reservoir and then through cooling coils to the second and third main reservoirs to the feed valve; which is set at 110 pounds pressure.

178

From feed valve through non-return check valve into the last main reservoir, from which branches lead to the brake valve, the brake application valve and master relay valve.

30. Q. What parts of the equipment are supplied with main reservoir air from the brake application valve?

A. The automatic brake pipe via the change over portion of the brake valve; also via chamber #25 above the application piston of the brake application valve and the safety control cut-out cock and to the throttle governor control.

31. Q. Name the parts that are furnished with main reservoir air at maximum pressure.

A. Main reservoir air gauge in control room; sanding devices on both power units, bell ringer, phneuphonic horn, compressor unloaders, high voltage control and automatic train control devices. With reducing valve set at 70 lbs., for H.V. cabnet and set at 60 lbs., for Automatic train control.

32. Q. What is the purpose of the control reservoir?

A. It is used in combination with the brake valve, a duplex circuit breaker and master relay valve, to provide a constant measuring volume when applying or releasing a straight air application of the brakes.

33. Q. What is the capacity of the control reservoir?

A. 436 cubic inches.

37. Q. How is the diaphragm flexed toward the application contactor?

A. By a higher air pressure in the control reservoir than what exists in the straight air pipe.

39. Q. What is the purpose of the master relay?

A. It is bolted to the same pipe bracket as the duplex circuit breaker and provides a means of applying and releasing the brakes, by the common straight air method, in case of failure of the electric circuits to control, pneumatically, the application and release magnets.

46. Q. What is the purpose of the volume reservoirs?

A. During an automatic application or when operating under the automatic brake system, air is admitted to the volume reservoirs from the auxiliary reservoirs and acts on the relay portion of the control valve to regulate the amount of air flowing to the brake cylinders.

72. Q. What are the functions of the BA-4 brake application valve?

A. Operates in response to a sudden reduction of brake pipe pressure to (a) close communication between the main reservoir supply pipe and the brake pipe; (b) provide an emergency brake application which is under control of the decelakron during the major portion of the stop;

A. (c) reduce brake pipe pressure to atmospheric; (d) cause a movement of the engine throttle to idling; (e) adjust the decelakron to provide a maximum rate of decelakron control throughout the stop.

73. Q. Why should communication between the main reservoir and automatic brake pipe be cut off after a sudden reduction of automatic brake pipe pressure?

A. To prevent loss of main reservoir air and prevent a possible recharge of the automatic brake pipe, thereby releasing the brake.

74. Q. Why close communication between brake pipe valve and control reservoir?

A. To permit main reservoir air to flow direct to stop cylinder of the decelakron and control reservoir.

75. Q. Would a safety control application, a conductor's valve application, or a broken automatic pipe produce this condition?

A. Yes.

76. Q. With anyone of the above brake applications in effect, would we have electric operation of the brakes?

A. Yes.

77. Q. How are the brakes applied under these conditions?

A. Main reservoir air will flow to the control reservoir and through a chokeplug of the BA-4 brake application valve and operate the duplex circuit breaker, applying the brakes electrically.

78. Q. If the brakes failed to apply electrically, how would they be applied?

A. Phneumatically, through the master relay valve (common straight air method).

179

128. Q. Why cannot a safety control application be released by depressing the foot pedal?

A. Because with the foot pedal depressed, the flow of main reservoir air from the brake valve to chamber #25 above the piston in the brake application valve will be blocked at the foot pedal.

136 Q. What would be the result if a break should occur in the straight air pipe while operating under the electro-pneumatic system?

A. An electric-pneumatic fast service brake application with the brake valve in service position.

137 Q. Why?

A. Due to the continual loss of straight air pipe pressure, the duplex circuit breaker would remain in contact with the application circuit, thereby keeping all application magnets energized.

145 Q. With a straight air electric application, are the brakes applied and released simultaneously throughout the train, or serially?

A. Simultaneously.

146. Q. How, with a straight air pneumatic application?

A. Serially--both application and release.

147 Q. Describe a straight air electric service application of the brakes.

A. Main reservoir air is admitted to the control reservoir via the decelakron. From the control reservoir it flows to the master relay and the duplex circuit breaker, forces master relay piston upward to close exhaust valve, and moves the circuit breaker to close contacts on the application magnet circuit energizing all application magnet valves throughout the train. The energized magnet valves now open to admit air, locally, from each supply reservoir to the straight air pipe. When pressure is established in the straight air pipe equal to that in the control reservoir, the circuit breaker moves to neutral position by reason of the equalized pressure on either side of its diaphragm, thus de-energizing the application magnets. As soon as any pressure is established in the straight air pipe it actuates the relay portion of each #22 control valve to admit air, locally, from the supply reservoirs to the brake cyclinders.

DUTIES ON ARRIVAL AT OAKLAND PIER

On arrival Oakland Pier westward trip, after stop is made, release straight air brakes, close cut out cock to brake valve, then change brake valve from straight to

automatic air, then make at least a 25 pound reduction and close double head cock, leaving brakes set for yard engine to release. This will eliminate the use of hand brakes. Return brake valve handle to running and remove reverse handle.

INSTRUCTIONS FOR OPERATING STEAM HEAT BOILERS

WARNING: Before starting steam generator, make sure that coil blow down valve #35 is closed, and boiler inlet feed water valve #36 is open.

1. Close main switch on wall, left side and start fuel pump.

2. See that the steam generator coils are filled with water. To fill steam generator coils press "FILL" and "START" switch buttons. When coils have been drained it takes about five (5) minutes to fill with rheostat in #20 position. To make sure that coils are filled open steam seperator blow down valve, then close same when water appears in the glass--coils are filled.

3. See that the safety #MB-# and high temperature #HH switches are in.

4. Open air atomizing valve #48 and set for 20 pounds atomizing pressure--better results are obtained by using air for atomizing--that will be the right hand valve.

5. Check to see that spark for ignition is working by looking in the peep hole.

6. Set theostat handle to No. 12 position.

7. When fuel pressure is up to above 50 pounds, press "GREEN" run switch button--fire should light immediately. When steam pressure builds up to whatever pressure is on steam heat line then open valve to train heat line.

8. Blow down steam seperator #CC to hold a half glass water. Leave seperator blow down #CMM open one half turn for five minutes, then open it wide and close it.

9. Adjust air on atomizer to burn a clean stack.

RUNNING ATTENTION

1. Once every hour give the steam seperator #CC a flash blow down and then use soot blower valves #22 and 23.

2. Also each hour turn handle on oil filter RR one full turn--clockwise.

3. Check feed water temperature by feeling the discharge pipe from the heat exchanger which should be 120 degrees temperature, hot to the touch or so you can just hold your hand on the pipe, if too hot or you cannot hold the pipe, too much water is being returned to the supply

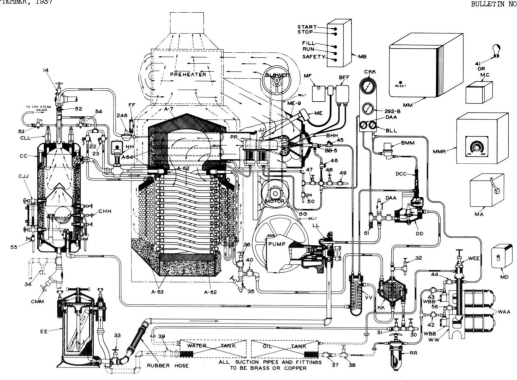

tank. Remedy; Increase fuel pressure—if too cold reduce fuel pressure.

fill steam generator before resetting, lower fuel pressure 10 pounds before restarting.

4.   If the high temperature switch #HH comes out,

5.   (this part unreadable on original copy) of the stack switch - #FF because of the stack too hot. The safety switch is set for ten seconds ignition delay—under no circumstances should this setting be changed.

6.   Three things will cause the boiler alarm to ring. First; operation of the electric cell, the contact must break. Second; the stack switch makes contact, it must be open. Third; The high temperature contact opens, that means not enough water being supplied.

When the boiler alarm rings, first press "FILL" button, then safety button, then check water pressure and fuel pressure and other devices such as ignition, fan belt slipping and atomizer. If bell rings again in a minute or so, check stack switch, photo-electric cell. See if contact is open or relay is energized.

<u>TO STOP STEAM GENERATOR UNIT</u>

Close the stop valve #14. This is all that is necessary for short stops. For longer stops, build the steam pressure up to 200 pounds, note if the pressure switch is set for a lower pressure, it can be held in contact by hand to build up the required pressure. Then press the "RED" stop switch button. With the blow off valve #35 blow the coil down until the steam pressure drops to 100 pounds.

Open blow off valve #CMM and blow down the steam seperator, then close the blow off valves, set the rheostat to No. 20 position, fill the steam generator by pressing the "FILL" and "GREEN" start switch buttons. Run until one inch of water shows in the glass.

Press the "RED" and "STOP" switch buttons. Open line switch #MA, the steam generator is now clean, filled with water and ready for use.

-13-

Appendix Three

SYNOPSIS

In accordance with a request from Mr. George McCormick of the Southern Pacific and instructions by Mr. H. L. Hamilton, Pres. of Electro-Motive Corp., the Metallurgical Department started an investigation on Sept. 6, 1939, into the conditions and relative damage done to gears and pinions of the "City of San Francisco" derailed at Harney, Nevada, on Aug. 12, 1939. Due to the general aspects of the problem, this investigation included also a rather general survey of the damage done to other parts such as trucks, motor frames, shafts, axles, wheels, etc.

The general view of the entire train after derailment and of the three locomotives are shown in the first two of these photographs. The bottom views of the equipment as received at the shops of Electro-Motive Corp. are given in the next illustrations. The notes on the bottom of each of these illustrations are self-explanatory. The detailed description of all gears and pinions are offered next. Although we have photographed the inside and outside of all gear cases as they reached the shops of Electro-Motive, we have positive proof that some of the dents on the gears do not correspond with those on the inside of the gear housings. This indicates definitely that they have were not replaced in the same sequence as they were at the time of the accident. The final section of this report covers the general views and detailed description of the motor frames removed. A few photographs covering the damage done to wheels are also offered. A summary on the general conditions of the integral parts and relative damage done is also presented on the large compilation:

LOCOMOTIVES — The markings of each unit by the joint owners is given in the center, the E-M serial number in the right corner, and the "F" in the left corner of each space reserved for every one of the three locomotives.

TRUCKS — The general index is given in the center, the truck No. of the General Steel Casting Corp. may be found in the lower left and the heat number in the lower right of each rectangle. The two ends are given below the first rectangle.

AXLES — "P" and "I" means power axle or idler axle. Location and identification marks are stamped on the end of the various axles found at the time the units were received at La Grange.

WHEELS — The wheels are given on both the right and left side in the same order in the trucks of the normal travel of the train.

GEARS — The stampings on the G. E. gears may be found in the attached description but for brevity we have offered only the actual serial numbers of each gear. "Left" and "Right" again indicates relative position on the locomotive. The dark area on each side of the number offers a relative idea of the scraped portion adjacent to the hubs of the gears.

PINIONS — Serial numbers and general conditions found by inspection are presented in the first two columns.

MOTOR SHAFTS — The twisting and measurable bending is given below conditions and indices of the pinions.

TRACTION MOTORS — The identification numbers are those to be found on the full page photographs of each of the motors. The motor number and armature number were taken from the proper portions of the assembly and may be correlated with Westinghouse Electric's data. The bottom view of each of these frames was then cut and placed in such order as to be interchangeable and showing the actual conditions under which the derailment caused markings in the lower-most portion of the motor frame.

In summing up these figures and pictures, it must be emphasized that the wheels, axles, and gear of number one end and number one truck were replaced after the accident. It should be borne in mind, therefore, that the area indicated in red should not be construed as part of the picture of the various parts of trucks involved in the derailment of the "City of San Francisco".

ELECTRO-MOTIVE CORPORATION
METALLURGICAL DEPARTMENT

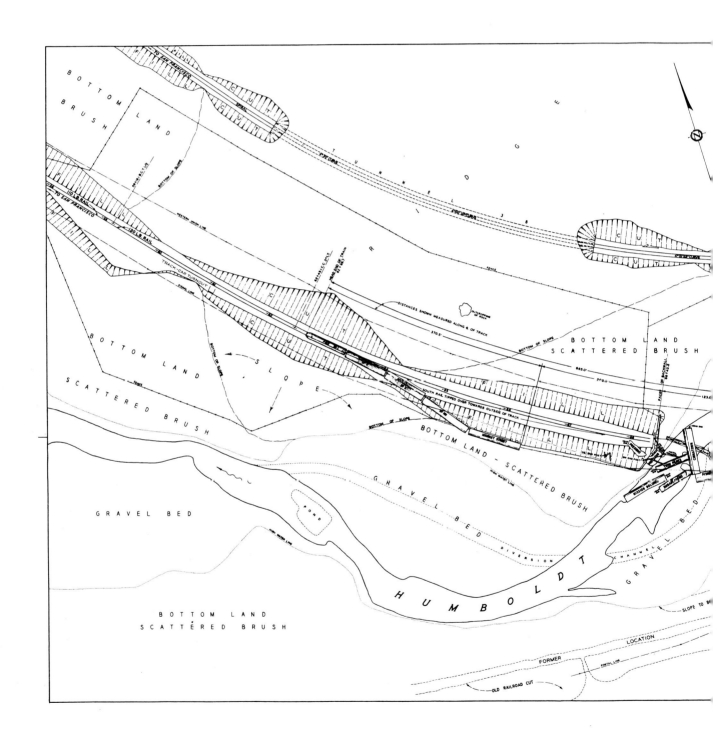

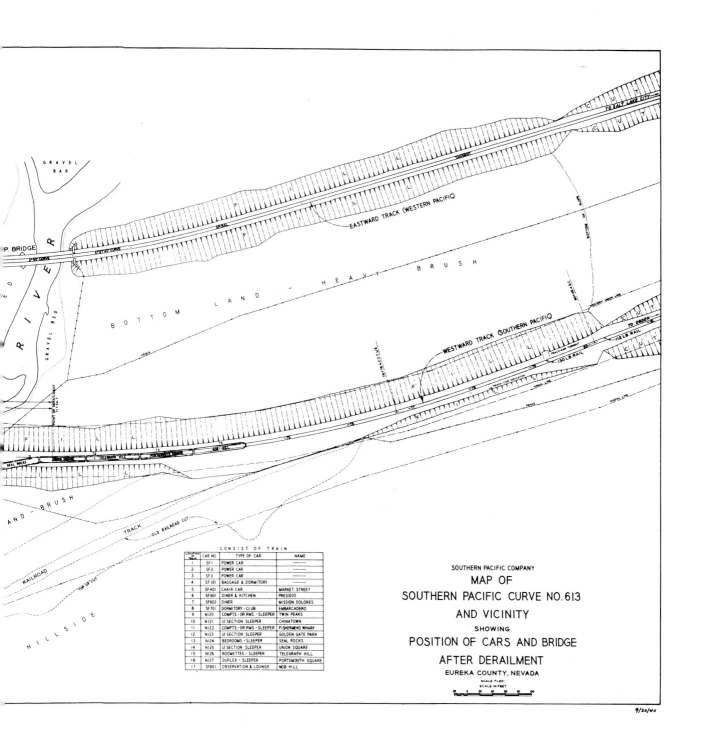

CONSIST OF TRAIN

LOCATION IN TRAIN	CAR NO.	TYPE OF CAR	NAME
1	SF1	POWER CAR	——
2	SF2	POWER CAR	——
3	SF3	POWER CAR	——
4	SF101	BAGGAGE & DORMITORY	——
5	SF401	CHAIR CAR	MARKET STREET
6	SF601	DINER & KITCHEN	PRESIDIO
7	SF602	DINER	MISSION DOLORES
8	SF701	DORMITORY - CLUB	EMBARCADERO
9	N120	COMPTS.- DR. RMS.- SLEEPER	TWIN PEAKS
10	N121	12 SECTION SLEEPER	CHINATOWN
11	N122	COMPTS.- DR. RMS.- SLEEPER	FISHERMENS WHARF
12	N123	12 SECTION SLEEPER	GOLDEN GATE PARK
13	N124	BEDROOMS - SLEEPER	SEAL ROCKS
14	N125	12 SECTION SLEEPER	UNION SQUARE
15	N126	ROOMETTES - SLEEPER	TELEGRAPH HILL
16	N127	DUPLEX - SLEEPER	PORTSMOUTH SQUARE
17	SF901	OBSERVATION & LOUNGE	NOB HILL

SOUTHERN PACIFIC COMPANY

MAP OF

SOUTHERN PACIFIC CURVE No. 613

AND VICINITY

SHOWING

POSITION OF CARS AND BRIDGE

AFTER DERAILMENT

EUREKA COUNTY, NEVADA

SCALE 1"=20'
SCALE IN FEET

9/20/40

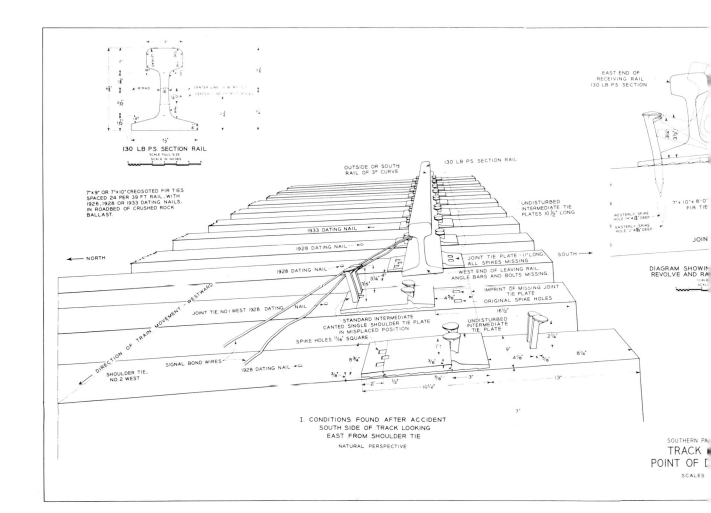

130 LB. P.S. SECTION RAIL
SCALE FULL SIZE
SCALE IN INCHES

7"x 9" OR 7"x 10" CREOSOTED FIR TIES
SPACED 24 PER 39 FT. RAIL, WITH
1926, 1928 OR 1933 DATING NAILS,
IN ROADBED OF CRUSHED ROCK
BALLAST.

OUTSIDE OR SOUTH
RAIL OF 3° CURVE

130 LB P.S. SECTION RAIL

EAST END OF
RECEIVING RAIL
130 LB P.S. SECTION

UNDISTURBED
INTERMEDIATE
TIE PLATES 10½" LONG

1933 DATING NAIL

1928 DATING NAIL

← NORTH

JOINT TIE PLATE - 11" LONG,
ALL SPIKES MISSING

SOUTH →

1928 DATING NAIL

WEST END OF LEAVING RAIL,
ANGLE BARS AND BOLTS MISSING.

IMPRINT OF MISSING JOINT
TIE PLATE
ORIGINAL SPIKE HOLES

WESTERLY SPIKE
HOLE "H" 4½" DEEP

EASTERLY SPIKE
HOLE "J" 4½" DEEP

7"x 10"x 8'-0"
FIR TIE

JOINT TIE NO.1 WEST 1928 DATING NAIL

STANDARD INTERMEDIATE
CANTED SINGLE SHOULDER TIE PLATE
IN MISPLACED POSITION

UNDISTURBED
INTERMEDIATE
TIE PLATE

DIAGRAM SHOWIN
REVOLVE AND RA

SPIKE HOLES 11/16" SQUARE

SIGNAL BOND WIRES

SHOULDER TIE,
NO.2 WEST

1928 DATING NAIL

I. CONDITIONS FOUND AFTER ACCIDENT
SOUTH SIDE OF TRACK LOOKING
EAST FROM SHOULDER TIE
NATURAL PERSPECTIVE

SOUTHERN PA
TRACK
POINT OF D
SCALES

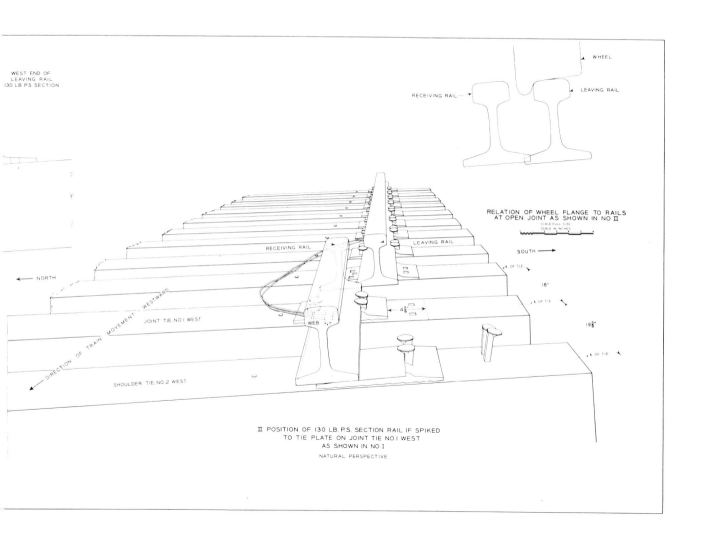

WEST END OF
LEAVING RAIL
130 LB. P.S. SECTION

WHEEL

RECEIVING RAIL

LEAVING RAIL

RELATION OF WHEEL FLANGE TO RAILS
AT OPEN JOINT AS SHOWN IN NO. II
SCALE FULL SIZE
SCALE IN INCHES

RECEIVING RAIL

LEAVING RAIL

SOUTH →

← NORTH

¢ OF TIE

18"

¢ OF TIE

19⅛"

¢ OF TIE

JOINT TIE, NO.I WEST

4⅝"

WEB

SHOULDER TIE, NO.2 WEST

II POSITION OF 130 LB. P.S. SECTION RAIL IF SPIKED
TO TIE PLATE ON JOINT TIE NO.I WEST
AS SHOWN IN NO. I

NATURAL PERSPECTIVE

187

STREAMLINER RESUMES RUN

Substituting for the train wrecked tragically in Nevada, the new streamlined "City of San Francisco," with a full load of passengers, sped on to the Oakland pier today on its first westbound run from Chicago.

The new train will start on its initial eastbound trip, on a 39¾-hour schedule, tomorrow. According to F. S. McGinnis, vice president of the Southern Pacific company, all accommodations have been sold out for a number of days.

Operated jointly by the Southern Pacific, Union Pacific and Chicago and North Western railroads, the train will continue in service on the Overland route until damaged equipment of the sabotaged train is replaced. It will depart from each terminal every six days.

Closely resembling the wrecked streamliner in appearance and color scheme, the new City of San Francisco is powered by a two-car Diesel-electric unit and carries 10 passenger cars and a baggage car.

Passenger equipment includes one coach, a two-car diner unit, six streamlined room sleeper cars and an observation-lounge car.

Pullman accommodations consist of 86 rooms, of which 35 are roomettes, five are drawing rooms, nine are compartments and 37 are bedrooms. All equipment is of the latest streamlined design.

NEW STREAMLINER ARRIVES

NEW STREAMLINED TRAIN, "City of San Francisco," substituting for Southern Pacific train wrecked in Nevada, arrived in Oakland today from east, all berths and seats taken. Left to right, J. O. Hand, engineer; G. E. Gaylord, superintendent western division, and Garnett King, assistant general passenger agent

—Post-Enquirer photo.